An American Constitution for Europe:

Reforming the European Union

By Jeffrey P. Cajka

Jeffrey P. Cajka

Acknowledgments

I would like to thank the Founders Constitution Website and the Rules and Procedures of the European Parliament Website for the invaluable information they provided.

Contents

Jeffrey P. Cajka

Preface

The European Union, formed under such optimism in 1993, foresaw a united, prosperous Europe, free of military conflict. That view has been muddied by the economic collapse of 2008, the revived aggressiveness of Russia and a refugee crisis that has divided the Union and caused Britain to begin the process of leaving the EU. Although the problems faced by the emerging United States after the American Revolution were different than the EU now faces, the forces threatening to collapse the EU were also present in America at that time.

This book offers a starting point for Europe to look at its problems as the 13 States looked at them in 1787. At the 1787 US Constitutional Convention, the delegates had a simple mission but a complex task: make their system of government stronger. Although there have been many criticisms of their work, the simple document they developed has lasted over two hundred years and served as a midwife to a country now the strongest and most prosperous on the planet.

In short, this book presents a proposed Constitution for The Federation of European Nations (FEN). Based on the US Constitution, the proposed document includes areas that appeal to Europeans and excludes those still causing problems in the US. But before we get to that proposed Constitution, it is seemly to review the problems the budding United States faced and the current EU must struggle with. Then we can review the proposed FEN Constitution as a solution.

The American colonies that rebelled against British rule in 1775 developed a unified form of government in 1777 known as the Articles of Confederation. The States gave up some of their sovereignty to a national government to help guarantee their liberty. Immediately, the conflict between supporting each State's freedom to operate and a national need to unite for common security caused problems that led to the abandonment of the Articles and development of the current US Constitution.

1

State Representation

The Congress of the Confederation was the only national government entity since no executive or judicial authority had been set up under the Articles. Each State could send 2-7 members, appointed by its Legislature to the Congress but each State was allowed only one vote on legislation. Like the nations of the European Union, each State was sovereign, i.e., it governed itself without interference from external powers. To ensure laws passed did not infringe on this sovereignty, 9 votes of 13 were needed to pass legislation. Consequently, each State had the same influence regardless of its wealth or population.

No taxing power

The biggest problem the United States faced under the Articles was funding. Because the cry of 'Taxation without Representation' was the main impetus for the Revolution, the States did not want to replace the taxing regime of George III with another national one. Although there was wide agreement that taxation was necessary, most agreed such power should be solely in the hands of the States. Consequently, under the Articles, the Congress had no power to tax.

If Congress needed money to pay for war or defend the country, it could either request funds from the States, borrow from foreign governments or sell western lands. Each State was supposed to contribute its share of expenses to a common treasury. Congress was supposed to decide the method of distributing each State's share. However, there was disagreement whether land or labor should be the basis of taxation, the heart of the unresolved issue of slavery.

The northern States argued that the shares should be based on the number of laborers, including slaves, in each state. Southern states countered by saying their slaves should not be counted because their slaves were property equivalent to other farm animals. To them, land was permanent and should be the basis of taxation, not laborers. Obviously, each State wanted the method resulting in the least expense to them. In any case, the taxes to provide these funds would be levied and collected by each State. Since the Congress could not force States to comply, many times the fund requisitions to the States were ignored.

Regulating Commerce

Although the Congress talked about the comradeship of the thirteen States, reality was that each State guarded its prerogatives and did what it thought best for its own interest. They were unwilling to see themselves as part of a greater nation and thus hamstrung Congress in many ways, especially around interstate trade, or interstate disputes. Although Congress had the authority to negotiate treaties with foreign governments, they could not control commerce between individual states and foreign countries.

Some States established duties on imported foreign goods even on goods from other States, required payment of tariffs in their own currency and even imposed competing tolls for traffic on rivers shared with other States. States without ports were at the mercy of States with ports which charged them transport costs. Each State had their own customs regulations and currencies confusing the consumer, the farmer and merchant and hampering trade.

Twelve of the 13 States wanted to give Congress the authority to regulate commerce but it needed an amendment to the Articles requiring unanimous approval. Rhode Island prevented the necessary change because it would have disrupted its habit of requiring its debt holders to accept its diminished currency in payment. The inability of Congress to control commerce led Maryland to call the Annapolis Convention which eventually led to the Constitutional Convention of 1787.

Enforcing Acts of Congress

The Articles did not establish a chief executive to enforce the laws or a national judiciary to interpret them. Congress chose one of its own to act as President annually but the person had no power except to preside at meetings. Since the Congress had no power to force the States to obey, the US found itself at a serious diplomatic disadvantage.

The Congress could declare war and call for an army, but it could not force the States to provide the troops or the equipment.

It needed funds from the States but could not force the States to give them. Congress could mediate between States but could not force a decision to be accepted, causing the whole governing process of the nation to become chaotic. States could not be forced to follow the Treaty of Paris ending the Revolution, and, in fact, they could enter into a treaty with a foreign government. The US could not even defend its borders against the British and Spanish but left it to the States to deal with the issues.

National Courts

The national government could not enforce its own laws since each State could interpret them to its own advantage or even ignore them. Disputes between States could not be settled because their courts favored them and there was no central court to give independent decisions. Without a supreme tribunal to expound and define the true meaning of the law, the law was useless, especially since the Congress had sole authority to settle boundary disputes and create courts to decide admiralty cases.

Article Amendments

"And the Articles of this confederation shall be inviolably observed by every State, and the union shall be perpetual; nor shall any alteration at any time hereafter be made in any of them; unless such alteration be agreed to in a congress of the United States, and be afterwards confirmed by the legislatures of every State."

To amend the Articles required unanimous approval of all 13 States. Although business prospered and population increased, problems requiring national action did not get resolved. The British still held territory in the Northwest by treaty was the property of the new United States.

National feeling grew that something needed to be done to provide a more effective union, but efforts to amend the articles to allow Congress tax authority failed in 1781 and 1786.

9/13 Rule

"The United States in Congress assembled shall never engage in a war, nor grant letters of marque or reprisal in time of peace, nor enter into any treaties or alliances, nor coin money, nor regulate the value thereof, nor ascertain the sums and expenses necessary for the defense and welfare of the United States, or any of them, nor emit bills, nor borrow money on the credit of the United States, nor appropriate money, nor agree upon the number of vessels of war, to be built or purchased, or the number of land or sea forces to be raised, nor appoint a commander in chief of the army or navy, unless nine States assent to the same..."

This clause showed the primacy of State power over the Congress. Nine out of thirteen states had to support a declaration of war, approve a treaty, issue currency, coin money, borrow money, appropriate money, procure a navy, raise an army, or appoint a commander in chief. Anything else needed a majority. In effect, 5 States could block an important bill. The five least populous States, Delaware, Rhode Island, New Hampshire, Georgia, and New Jersey had less population combined than Virginia. But those five States could block any legislation of Congress helping many Americans.

National Defense

Note that the Congress was set up to prosecute the Revolution by setting up a Continental Army, obtain reinforcements from State militias, request funds from the States to pay for the war and conduct a foreign policy to support the Revolution. Although only Congress could declare war and raise an army, it could not force any State to provide troops or the arms and equipment needed to support them despite each State having a well-regulated, disciplined, and supplied militia.

Nevertheless, George Washington was left to deal with these problems because Congress was unable to perform its functions. It is a testament to Washington that the Army he assembled, trained, and supplied could survive until victory. He often had to defer strategic actions to deal with 13 State governments for supplies and troops. After the war was over, the British broke the treaty ending the war several times, but the Congress could not protect American rights under the treaty. The national government could not even put down an internal rebellion against taxation, known as Shay's Rebellion.

Currency Control

Article IX of the Articles of Confederation states, "The United States in Congress assembled shall also have the sole and exclusive right and power of regulating the alloy and value of coin struck by their own authority, or by that of the respective State." So, both Congress and the States could issue currency. Since all did, there was no single currency, and chaos prevailed as trade between States and with foreign governments became difficult. For example, seven States printed large quantities of paper money, having questionable value, to pay their veterans, creditors and to settle debts between their citizens.

No National Tariffs

Taxation was the province of the States and even tariffs were prohibited to the Congress. Consequently, the States enacted tariffs even between themselves and other States. Since the Congress had no power to regulate commerce, the States began bitter tariff wars among themselves. Foreign countries refused to work with Congress on commercial trade agreements because they knew the Congress had no authority to enforce them.

If we look at the current EU, we can see some of the same issues. When a crisis arrives, whatever the source, policies designed and leaders chosen in calmer times do not handle the enormous pressures and cast doubt on the underlying structures political and economic.

Control of Immigration

More than 1 million refugees streaming into Europe in 2015 laid bare the ineffective immigration policies of the EU and highlighted the divisions among member Nations. The open border policy within the EU (Schengen) was satisfactory in normal times but collapsed when faced with a huge influx of refugees escaping war. Schengen places the burden of refugee processing on the country where refugees first arrive, in this case, Greece and Italy.

Faced with the huge influx, Italy and Greece gave up and allowed the refugees to move on to other EU nations, even those not in the EU, to deal with. Frontex, the EU institution tasked to handle border control was not funded or staffed properly to handle the problem. Member nations also violated Schengen principles by building fences or reestablishing border controls to prevent the entrance of refugees. Former Eastern Bloc countries were hostile to refugees and tried to keep them out. Western European countries accepted refugees but some national leaders like Germany's Chancellor aggravated the situation by welcoming refugees, which encouraged more to leave their war-torn countries.

Combined with the Eurozone financial crisis, the refugee problem threatened to split the EU. Each nation's leaders looked at the problem in how it affected his or her domestic program. Right wing parties in some nations gained strength in harvesting the resentment of its populace. Backlash from refugee demands on social and educational services were causing xenophobic tendencies. Despite the resistance to refugees settling in their nations, the low birthrates in most EU countries need immigrants for economic growth.

Budgetary control of countries with a common currency

In 1992, EU member nations signed the Maastricht Treaty where they pledged to limit deficit spending and debt. Since the new millennium began, several nations did not follow these strictures and accumulated excessive debt because of easy credit availability. The financial crisis of 2007-08, trade imbalances, real estate bubbles and the Great Recession caused a debt crisis wherein government defaults and downgraded bond ratings affected several EU nations, beginning with Greece, and spreading to Ireland and Portugal.

These nations could not refinance their debt without help from other EU nations or the IMF. But the help came with strict austerity measures that increased unemployment and caused recession in the affected nation. Normally a nation facing a debt crisis can devalue its currency to pay the debt with lower valued money. Since the EU has a unified currency, the Euro, that option was off the table, eventually starting a crisis affecting labor markets and economic growth over the entire EU.

All laws passed by the EU must be passed and implemented in each nation

EU law has equal force with national law. However, each member nation must implement EU law in national law and enforce it. The EU Commission monitors the application of EU law and can refer an offending member nation to the European Court of Justice.

Amendments to the EU Treaty require unanimous agreement

Treaties underlying the EU can be changed in 3 ways. First, the traditional method requires a change proposal from an EU Institution to the European Council. The President of the EU can then either call a Convention of all national governments to draft the changes needed or direct the Council to draft the proposal. Changes are then approved by an Intergovernmental conference and sent to all national leaders for ratification by each nation.

Second, a simplified revision process was set up by the Treaty of Lisbon that only allows changes not increasing the EU's authority. Under this process, the European Council can approve the change but it still must be ratified by all Nations. The third option, the Passarelle clause in the treaty, allows amending the treaties to change legislative procedure if the European Council unanimously agrees but cannot be used in areas affecting defense.

No central military control

The armed forces of the EU are composed of the structures set up between armed forces of the member nations and the Common Security and Defence Policy (CSDP). However, each member nation has its own defense policy complicated by the main military alliance of NATO which includes 22 of the EU nations plus four European nations not in the EU along with the US and Canada.

Treaties underlying the EU call for military integration within the EU, but full integration requires unanimous approval of the European Council. The suggestion has been opposed by several member nations, but the confrontation with Russia over Ukraine has enhanced the discussion. Although the EU is running 6 military missions and 11 civilian operations now, those serving are part of member nation forces not an EU army.

Some EU nations issue their own currency

The EU set up a path for a unified multinational financial system under a single currency. Initially, the Euro ended exchange rate fluctuations between national currencies, increased price transparency and unified the market. Most original EU nations chose to adopt the Euro but some (Denmark, Sweden, and the UK) declined. Now only 19 of the 28 EU nations use the Euro, but all, except the United Kingdom and Denmark, must eventually adopt the Euro.

Some believe European countries are too diverse economically to share in a common currency. However, the diversity is not more variable than the States in the US where a common currency has been in effect for two centuries. The problem is that EU member Nations are in full control of their budgets and dominate government spending in the EU, while much of the government spending in the US is conducted by the federal government. Even those US States or cities having debt problems cannot damage the US or demand a bailout from the federal government. Moreover, 49 US States have constitutional requirements to balance their budgets in some form.

While countries using the common currency agreed to limit their deficits, there was no penalty if they did not comply. The only solution to the problem was to forgive some of the debt in return for austerity provisions on the non-complying country. Greece was forced to cut pensions, raise taxes, and sell assets. Although the threat of these measures was the solution for countries not complying, unless economic policy is enforced on a continuing basis, the shared currency system will not survive.

Diversity of the member nation economies can cause problems. The European Central Bank (ECB), the central bank for the Eurozone economies, can hurt some nations as it helps others. For example, when Germany experienced high inflation, the ECB raised interest rates which hurt Italy and Portugal.

EU nations that have not adopted the Euro do so to maintain economic independence:

- A nation can set its own fiscal and monetary policies independent of the European Central Bank. In effect, it can cut interest rates and begin quantitative easing to overcome economic downturns.
- They have their own central bank, the lender of last resort for the country's debt that can buy bonds to increase liquidity in the money market. If inflation occurs, they can raise interest rates.
- Currency devaluation can help a nation deal with reduced exports or production and high debt by making exports cheaper and encouraging foreign investment.

The FEN Constitution on the following pages attempts to set up a government for Europe that will provide common security and preserve each Nation's sovereignty. The conclusion to this book shows the steps the Separate American States took to set up a nation 'of the people, by the people and for the people,' and the steps the EU might take to set up a similar European nation.

The Proposed Constitution of the Federation of European Nations

W e, the People of the European Union, in order to: promote peace; maintain freedom, security, and justice; develop and maintain an internal commercial market; sustain economic development; promote social justice and equality; and ensure territorial cohesion and respect for linguistic and cultural diversity, establish this Constitution for the Federation of European Nations.

Chapter I – The European Assembly
Article 1 – Legislative Powers

All legislative powers granted herein shall be vested in a European Assembly, which shall consist of two Houses: a Senate and Chamber of Delegates.

Article 2 – The Chamber of Delegates

1. The Chamber of Delegates shall be composed of Members chosen every four years by the people of each Federation Nation. The People in each Nation shall have the same eligibility in voting for Delegates as they have in voting for the most numerous branch of their Nation's Legislature.

2. A Delegate must be at least 25 years old at the time of election, have been a Citizen of a Federation Nation for at least 10 years, and must have been a resident of the Nation he or she represents for at least one year prior to the time of election.

3. Each Nation in this Federation shall have a number of Delegates based on its population, excluding non-citizens. A population census shall be made within three years after the first meeting of the European Assembly, and every ten years thereafter, according to rules that the Assembly shall establish by law. The total number of Chamber Delegates shall not exceed 400 but each Nation shall have at least one Delegate. Until the first census takes place, the Nations ratifying this Constitution shall have the following number of Delegates: Austria shall be entitled to elect seven, Belgium nine, Bulgaria six, Cyprus one, Czech Republic eight, Denmark four, Estonia one, Finland four, France fifty-two,

Germany sixty-five, Greece nine, Hungary eight, Ireland four, Italy forty-eight, Latvia two, Lithuania three, Luxembourg one, Malta one, Netherlands thirteen, Poland thirty-one, Portugal eight, Romania fifteen, Slovakia four, Slovenia two, Spain thirty-seven, Sweden seven, and the United Kingdom fifty.

4. When a vacancy occurs in the representation of any Nation in the Chamber, the Head of that Nation's government shall ensure a by-election occurs to fill the vacancy within 30 days.

5. The Chamber of Delegates shall choose its Speaker and other officers, and shall have the sole power of impeachment.

Article 3 – The European Senate

1. The Senate shall be composed of four Senators from each Nation, elected by the People thereof, for eight years, each Senator having one vote in the Senate. The People in each Nation shall have the same eligibility in voting for Senators as they have in voting for the most numerous branch of their Nation's Legislature.

2. In the first election of Senators, each Nation will assign one of its Senators a term of two years, another four years, another six years and the last the full eight years. In subsequent elections, all Senators will have a term of eight years. The purpose of this procedure is to ensure that one-quarter of the Senate will face election every two years. When a vacancy occurs in the representation of any Nation in the Senate, the Head of that Nation's government shall ensure a by-election occurs to fill the vacancy within 90 days.

3. A Senator must be at least 30 years old at the time of election, have been a Citizen of a Federation Nation for at least 10 years, and must be a resident of the Nation he or she represents for at least one year prior to the time of election.

4. The Vice President of the Federation shall be President of the Senate, but shall have no vote, unless it is equally divided. When there is a vacancy in the office of the Vice President, the Vice President is Acting

President or unable to serve, the Senate shall appoint a President pro tempore from among its members to preside. The Senate shall choose its other officers.

5. The Senate shall have the sole power to try all impeachments. When the President or Vice President of the Federation is being tried, the Chairman of the European Supreme Court will preside. A vote of two-thirds of Senators present will constitute a conviction and immediate removal from office.

6. The penalty for an impeachment conviction can only be removal from office and disqualification from further office under the Federation, but the convicted shall still be liable for indictment, trial, judgment, and punishment under law.

Article 4 – Elections to the Assembly

1. Each Nation's Legislature shall decide the time, place, and manner of elections to the Chamber and Senate, but the Assembly may, by law, make or change such decisions.

2. The terms of Senators and Delegates shall end at noon on the 8th day of April of the year the term is to end, when the terms of their successors will begin.

3. The Assembly shall convene at least once every year beginning at noon on the 8th day of April unless it selects a different day, by law.

Article 5 – Legislative Procedures

1. Each House shall be the judge of the election and qualifications of its own Members, a majority of which shall constitute a quorum to conduct business. If a quorum does not exist, Members can be compelled to attend in a manner and with penalties as each House may establish.

2. Each House may determine its own rules of procedure, discipline its Members, and, with the concurrence of two thirds, expel a Member.

3. Each House shall keep a journal of its proceedings and publish it weekly when in session, excluding items that, in its judgment, affect Federation security. The journal shall include the votes of the Members of each House by name on all questions unless a majority of the House present objects.

4. Neither House, during an Assembly session, shall adjourn for more than one week, nor to any other place than that in which the two Houses are sitting, without the consent of the other House.

Article 6 – Compensation, Privileges, and Restrictions

1. Senators and Delegates shall receive compensation for their services from the Federation Treasury according to law. They cannot be arrested or detained while en route to or from a session of their respective Houses, except for treason or felony. Any speech or debate occurring during a House session shall not be questioned in any other place.

2. Senators and Delegates, during their terms of election, shall not accept or serve in any civil office of the Federation. A Person serving in any civil office of the Federation must resign that position before standing for election to the Assembly.

3. No law varying the compensation for the services of the Senators and Delegates shall take effect until an election of Delegates shall have intervened.

Article 7 – Legislative Bills

1. All bills for raising revenue shall originate in the Chamber of Delegates. The Senate may agree to, or decrease the amount of revenue in a bill but shall not increase the amount or add revenue by amending another bill. Other bills from the Chamber can be amended or concurred with by the Senate. The Senate may initiate bills that do not raise revenue.

2. Every bill that passes the Chamber of Delegates and the Senate shall be provided to the President of the Federation. If the President approves it, he or she shall sign it and it will become law. If the

President does not approve it, it will be returned to the House it originated from, along with the President's reasons for disapproval. The House will enter the President's reasons into its journal and reconsider the bill. If, after reconsideration, two thirds of the House agrees to pass the bill, it will be sent to the other House along with the President's reasons for disapproval. The other House will proceed in a like manner to reconsider the bill and if passed by two thirds of that House, it shall become law. In such cases, all votes shall be recorded in the journal of each House and the names of the Members voting for and against the bill shall be recorded. If a bill is not returned by the President to the Assembly within 10 days after submittal to him or her, it shall become law, unless the Assembly has prevented its return by adjournment.

3. All orders, resolutions, or votes that require the concurrence of the Senate and Chamber of Delegates, except for adjournment or amendments to this Constitution, shall be provided to the President of the Federation for approval before they can take effect. If such orders, resolutions, or votes are not approved, they may be repassed by a vote of two thirds of the Senate and Chamber of Delegates according to the same rules prescribed for a bill.

Article 8 – Legislative Powers

The Assembly shall have power:

1. To impose and collect taxes, import duties, and excises and pay the debts and fund the common defense and general welfare of the Federation, but all import duties, and excises shall be uniform throughout the Federation;

2. To borrow money on the credit of the Federation, the validity of which, as authorized by law, shall not be questioned;

3. To regulate commerce with foreign countries and among the Nations of the Federation;

4. To establish uniform laws of Citizenship, immigration, naturalization, and bankruptcies throughout the Federation;

5. To produce Federation coin and currency, to regulate their value and that of foreign currency, and to establish the Federation standard of weights and measures;

6. To prescribe measures to prevent counterfeiting of the securities, coin and currency of the Federation;

7. To establish and maintain a postal service;

8. To promote innovation and research by establishing laws for copyrights, patents, trademarks, and other intellectual property;

9. To define and punish piracies, crimes committed in international waters, and violations of international law;

10. To authorize and limit the use of military force and establish rules concerning prisoners of war and captured property;

11. To create and support a Federation Armed Force for defense of the Federation and its Nations;

12. To make rules for managing the Federation Armed Force;

13. To provide rules for summoning the Armed Forces of Federation Nations to execute the laws of the Federation, suppress insurrections, and repel invasions;

14. To provide rules for organizing, arming, and disciplining the Armed Forces of Federation Nations and for governing them when in the service of the Federation, reserving to each Nation the appointment of officers, and training of its Armed Forces according to the discipline prescribed by the European Assembly;

15. To exercise legislative authority in all cases over the seat of government, not to exceed five contiguous square miles, within which no Person shall take up residence, that is ceded by a Nation and accepted by the European Assembly;

16. To limit, regulate, and prohibit the labor of Persons less than eighteen years of age;

17. To exercise exclusive legislative authority in all cases over real property acquired for the needs of the Federation with the consent of the affected Nation's Legislature; and,

18. To legislate where necessary and proper to execute the foregoing powers and all other powers provided in this Constitution to the government of the Federation, its offices or officers.

Article 9 – Limits on the European Assembly

1. An order requiring a Person under arrest to be brought before a judge, known otherwise as a writ of habeas corpus, shall not be suspended unless the safety of the public requires it in the case of rebellion or invasion.

2. No legislative act that singles out an individual or group for punishment without a trial, known otherwise as a bill of attainder, shall be passed.

3. No retroactive law, known otherwise as an ex post facto law, shall be passed.

4. No tax or duty shall be imposed on items exported from any Federation Nation.

5. No regulatory or revenue law shall give preference to the ports of one Federation Nation over another; nor shall any Federation Nation impose an import duty on items imported from any other Federation Nation.

6. No money shall be disbursed from the Treasury, unless appropriated by the Assembly in law. An annual accounting of Federation revenues and disbursements shall be published.

7. No title of nobility shall be granted by the Federation; and no Person holding any office under the Federation shall accept any gift, office, or title of any kind from any monarch, or foreign country without the consent of the European Assembly.

8. The Assembly shall make no laws establishing or supporting a religion or religions, or prohibiting the free exercise thereof, or abridging the

freedom of speech, or the press, or the right of the People to assemble peaceably and to petition the government for a redress of grievances.

9. The right of the People to be secure in their Persons, houses, papers, and effects against unreasonable searches and seizures shall not be violated. No search or arrest warrant shall be issued but upon probable cause, supported by oath or affirmation, particularly describing the place to be searched and the Persons or things to be seized.

10. No Person shall be held to answer for a crime that may result in incarceration without an indictment by a grand jury, except for Persons on active duty in the Armed Forces. Moreover, no Person shall be subject to more than one trial for the same offence, or be compelled in any criminal case to be a witness against himself or herself, or be deprived of life, liberty, or property without due process of law. Private property shall not be taken for public use without just compensation.

11. In all criminal prosecutions, the accused shall have a speedy and public trial by an impartial jury composed of Citizens of the Nation and district where the crime was committed, the district having been previously established by law. The accused shall be informed of the nature and cause of the accusation, have the opportunity to confront the prosecution witnesses, have a compulsory process for obtaining witnesses in his or her favor, and have the assistance of legal counsel for his or her defense. All criminal convictions shall require a unanimous jury verdict.

12. In civil lawsuits where the value in controversy exceeds an amount determined by the Assembly, the right of trial by jury shall be preserved, and no fact tried by a jury shall be otherwise re-examined in any court of the Federation unless a retrial is conducted.

13. Excessive bail shall not be required, nor excessive fines imposed, nor cruel and unusual punishments inflicted, all as defined by the Assembly in law. The death penalty shall not be imposed by the Federation, or by any Member Nation or other jurisdiction within the Federation.

14. The enumeration in this Constitution of certain rights shall not be interpreted as denying or disparaging others retained by the People of the Federation.

15. The powers not given to the Federation by this Constitution, nor prohibited by it to Federation Nations, are reserved for the Nations or for the People of the Federation.

Article 10 – Limits on Federation Nations

1. No Nation shall enter into any treaty, alliance or confederation, coin money or issue currency, make anything but Federation currency or coin legal tender, pass any retroactive law, or a law that singles out an individual or group for punishment without a trial, or a law that impairs the obligations of a legal contract.

2. No Nation shall impose a duty on imports, exports, or weight beyond those charges necessary to fund the basic cost of its inspection laws without the approval of the Assembly. All such charges shall be subject to the control of the Assembly.

3. No Nation shall, without the consent of the Assembly, keep an Armed Force independent of the Federation Armed Forces nor enter into any agreement with another Federation Nation or foreign power, nor engage in war unless invaded or in imminent danger of invasion.

4. The right of Federation Citizens who are 18 years of age or older, to vote, shall not be denied or reduced by the Federation or a Member Nation because of race, color, gender, religious belief, or failure to pay any tax.

5. No money raised by taxation in any Nation for the support of public schools, or derived from any public fund for that purpose, nor any public lands devoted thereto, shall ever be under the control of any religious sect; nor shall any money so raised or lands so devoted be provided to religious sects or denominations.

Chapter II – The Executive
Article 1 – The President and Vice President

1. The executive power shall be vested in a President of the Federation of European Nations. The President shall hold the office for a term of six

years, and, together with the Vice President, chosen for the same term, shall be elected as follows:

a. Each Nation shall select, based on rules established by its Legislature, a number of Electors, equal to the number of Senators and Delegates they are entitled to in the European Assembly. The Assembly may determine the schedule for choosing the Electors, and their voting day that shall be uniform throughout the Federation. No Senator, Delegate, or Person holding office of any kind under the Federation, or Person not born in the respective Nation shall be appointed an Elector.

b. The Electors shall meet in their respective Nations and vote by ballot for President and Vice-President, one of whom, at least, shall not have been born in the same Nation as themselves. They shall name in one ballot the Person voted for as President, and in another ballot the Person voted for as Vice President, and they shall make separate lists of all Persons voted for as President, and of all Persons voted for as Vice President, and of the number of votes for each. The Electors shall sign and certify the lists and transmit them sealed to the seat of the government of the Federation of European Nations, directed to the Speaker of the Chamber of Delegates.

c. The Speaker of the Chamber, in the presence of the Senators and Delegates, shall open all the certified lists and the votes shall then be counted. The Person having the greatest number of votes for President shall be the President, if the number of votes is a majority of the whole number of Electors appointed. If no Person has such a majority, then from the Persons having the three highest numbers of votes on the list of those voted for as President, the Chamber shall choose immediately, by ballot, the President. However, in choosing the President, the votes shall be taken by Nations, the representation from each Nation having one vote. A quorum for this purpose shall consist of at least one Delegate from two-thirds of the Nations, and a majority of all the Nations shall be necessary to a choice.

d. The Person having the greatest number of votes for Vice President shall be the Vice President, if the number of votes is a majority of the whole number of Electors appointed. If no Person has a majority, then from the Persons having the two highest numbers of votes on the list of those voted for as Vice President, the Senate shall choose the Vice President. A quorum for the purpose shall consist of two-thirds of the whole number of Senators, and a majority of the whole number shall be necessary to a choice.

e. The Assembly may, by law, provide for the case of the death of any of the Persons from whom the Assembly may choose as President whenever the right of choice shall have devolved upon them, and for the case of the death of any of the Persons from whom the Senate may choose as Vice President whenever the right of choice shall have devolved upon them.

f. If a President has not been chosen before the time fixed for the beginning of the President's term, the Vice President-elect shall act as President until a President has been chosen. The Assembly may, by law, provide for the case wherein neither a President-elect or a Vice President-elect has been chosen, declaring who shall then act as President, or the manner in which one is to act shall be selected, and such Person shall act accordingly until a President or Vice President has been chosen.

2. No Person constitutionally ineligible to the office of President shall be eligible to that of Vice President and no Person shall be elected to the office of the President more than twice.

3. The President must have been born in a Federation Nation, must be 35 years old at the time of election, and must have been a resident of a Federation Nation for at least 15 years.

4. The President shall receive a salary set by the Assembly that cannot be increased or decreased during the President's term of office. The President shall not receive within that term of office any other compensation or gift from the Federation or any of its Nations.

5. Before assuming the duties of the office, the President shall take the following oath or affirmation in the presence of the Assembly: "I do solemnly swear (or affirm) that I will faithfully execute the Office of President of the Federation of European Nations, and will, to the best of my ability, preserve, protect, and defend the Constitution of the Federation of European Nations."

6. The terms of the President and Vice President shall end at noon on the 8th day of May of the year the term is to end, when the terms of their successors will begin. If, at the time fixed for the beginning of the term of the President, the President-elect shall have died, the Vice President-elect shall become President.

7. If the President is removed from office, dies, resigns, or is unable to discharge the powers and duties of the office, the Vice President shall become President. The Assembly, by law, may provide a further line of succession in case of removal, death, resignation, or inability to discharge the powers and duties of the office, of both the President and Vice President. In no case, however, will a by-election be held to fill a vacancy in the Presidential office.

8. Whenever there is a vacancy in the office of the Vice President, the President shall nominate a Vice President who shall take office upon confirmation by a majority vote of both Houses of the Assembly.

9. Whenever the President transmits to the Vice President and the Speaker of the Chamber of Delegates a written declaration that he or she is unable to discharge the powers and duties of the office, and until he or she transmits to them a written declaration to the contrary, such powers and duties shall be discharged by the Vice President as Acting President.

10. Whenever the Vice President and a majority of either the principal officers of the executive departments, or of such other body as the Assembly may by law provide, transmit to the Senate and the Speaker of the Chamber of Delegates their written declaration that the President is unable to discharge the powers and duties of his or her office, the Assembly shall decide the issue, meeting within forty-eight hours for that purpose. If the Assembly, within twenty-one days after receipt of the latter written declaration, determines by two-thirds vote of both Houses that the President is unable to discharge the powers and duties of his or her office, the Vice President shall discharge the same as Acting President; otherwise, the President shall continue to execute the powers and duties of his or her office. If, after such determination, the President transmits to the President pro tempore of the Senate and the Speaker of the Chamber of Delegates his or her written declaration that

no inability exists, the Assembly shall decide the issue, meeting within forty-eight hours. If the Assembly, within twenty-one days after receipt of the President's written declaration, determines by two-thirds vote of both Houses that the President is able to discharge the powers and duties of his or her office, the President shall resume the powers and duties of his or her office; otherwise, the Vice President shall remain Acting President.

Article 2 – Presidential Powers

1. The President shall be Commander in Chief of the Armed Forces of the Federation and of any Armed Force of a Federation Nation when called into the actual service of the Federation. The President shall exercise executive authority over the executive departments and shall have power to grant reprieves and pardons for offences against the Federation, except for Impeachment.

2. The President shall have power to make treaties or executive agreements that shall have the force of law, provided two thirds of the Senators concur. With the concurrence of a majority of Senators, the President shall appoint Ambassadors, other public ministers and Consuls, Judges of the Supreme Court, and all other officers of the Federation whose appointments are not herein otherwise provided for, and are established by law. The Assembly, by law, may provide the power of appointment of subordinate officers to the President, his or her subordinates, or to the Judiciary without Senate approval.

3. All Presidential appointments that, by law, must be approved by the Senate shall be voted on by the Senate within 90 days of submittal by the President or they shall be considered confirmed.

Article 3 – Presidential Responsibilities

The President, in the presence of the Assembly, shall annually address the People on the state of the Federation and recommend legislation to further Federation goals as expressed in the Preamble to this Constitution. The President shall have authority to call the Assembly into special session to address extraordinary problems. The President may adjourn the Assembly in case of disagreement between the two Houses on the time of adjournment. The President, as Head of State, shall receive Ambassadors and other public ministers, ensure that the laws are executed in good faith, and shall commission all the officers of the Federation.

Article 4 – Impeachment

The President, Vice President, Judges, and all civil officers of the Federation, as defined by law, shall be removed from office on Impeachment for, and conviction of, treason, bribery, perjury, abuse of authority, obstruction of justice, dereliction of duty, or other felonies.

Chapter III – The Judiciary
Article 1 – Federation Courts

The judicial power of the Federation shall be placed in one Supreme Court and in such subordinate courts as the Assembly may establish. The Judges, both of the Supreme and subordinate courts, shall hold their offices for life, unless removed by impeachment and conviction, or resignation, and shall receive for their services a compensation that shall not be diminished during their tenure even if the Assembly abolishes the court on which they serve.

Article 2 – Judicial Power, Jurisdiction and Trial by Jury

1. The Judicial Power of the Federation of European Nations shall be over: all cases that arise under this Constitution, the laws of the Federation, and treaties and executive agreements made under its authority; all cases involving Ambassadors, Consuls and other ministers performing diplomatic functions; all cases of admiralty and maritime jurisdiction; controversies in which the Federation is a party; and controversies between Federation Nations, between Citizens of different Federation Nations, and between Citizens of the same Federation Nation claiming property in a different Federation Nation.

2. The Supreme Court shall have original jurisdiction in all cases affecting Ambassadors, Consuls, and other ministers performing

diplomatic functions, and those in which a Federation Nation shall be a party. In all other cases under its authority, the Supreme Court shall have appellate jurisdiction, in law and fact, under such rules the Assembly shall make.

3. The trial of all crimes, except in cases of impeachment, shall be by jury and be held in the Federation Nation where the alleged crime was committed. When the crime was not committed within any Federation Nation, the trial shall take place where the Assembly, by law, has directed.

Article 3 – Treason

1. Treason against the Federation of European Nations shall consist only in levying war against it or giving aid to its enemies. Conviction for treason requires the testimony of two witnesses to the same overt act or open confession in court.

2. The Assembly shall have power to prescribe the punishment for treason.

Chapter IV – Government Relationships
Article 1 – Full Faith and Credit

Each Nation shall recognize and enforce the public acts, records, and judicial proceedings of every other Nation. The Assembly, by law, may prescribe the manner in which such acts, records, and proceedings shall be proved, and their effect.

Article 2 – Obligations of Federation Nations

1. A Federation Nation may not deprive the Citizens of another Federation Nation the privileges and immunities that its own Citizens enjoy, including but not limited to: protection by the government; the enjoyment of life and liberty; the right to travel through and reside in any other Federation Nation; the right to engage in commerce, agriculture, the professions or other occupation; the privilege of a writ

requiring a Person under arrest to be brought before a judge; the right to institute action in any court; the right to obtain, hold and dispose of real and personal property; and, exemption from higher taxes than are paid by Citizens of the Federation Nation.

2. A Person charged in any Nation with treason, felony, or other crime, who shall flee from justice and be found in another Nation, shall, on demand of the Head of Government from which he or she fled, be delivered up to the Nation having jurisdiction of the crime.

3. Slavery or involuntary servitude, except as punishment for a crime for which the party has been duly convicted, shall not exist within the Federation or any place subject to its jurisdiction.

4. A Person born in a Federation Nation and having one parent who was born in a Federation Nation, subject to its jurisdiction, or a Person naturalized within the Federation, is a Citizen of the Federation and the Nation wherein he or she resides. No Nation shall make or enforce any law that abridges the privileges or immunities of Citizens of the Federation, nor shall any Nation deprive any Person of life, liberty, or property, without due process of law, nor deny to any Person within its jurisdiction the equal protection of the laws.

Article 3 – Additions to the Federation and Control of Federation Property

1. Foreign countries may be admitted by the Assembly into this Federation with the same status, rights, and obligations as existing Federation Nations. However, no foreign country shall be admitted that is under the jurisdiction of any other Federation Nation or foreign country. Moreover, no Federation Nation shall be created by the merger of two or more Federation Nations, or parts of Federation Nations, without the consent of the Legislatures of the Nations concerned as well as of the Assembly.

2. The Assembly shall have power to make all rules and regulations over the territory or other property belonging to the Federation; and nothing

in this Constitution shall be so construed as to prejudice any claims of the Federation, or of any particular Federation Nation.

Article 4 – Obligations of the Federation

The Federation shall guarantee to every Federation Nation a Republican form of government, shall protect each of them against invasion, and upon request of its Legislature or of its Head of Government (when the Legislature cannot be convened), against domestic violence. The Assembly shall be the sole judge of whether a Nation has a republican form of government and shall confirm that judgment by acceptance or rejection of Delegates or Senators from that Nation by either House.

Chapter V – Amendments to this Constitution

This Constitution can be amended in two ways. First, whenever two thirds of both Houses shall deem it necessary, the Assembly shall propose Amendments to this Constitution; or, secondly, when the Legislatures of two thirds of Federation Nations shall call for a Convention to propose Amendments. In either case, the Amendments shall be valid to all intents and purposes, as part of this Constitution, when ratified by either the Legislatures of three fourths of Federation Nations, or by Conventions in three fourths thereof, as determined by the Assembly. However, no Federation Nation, without its consent, shall be deprived of its equal representation in the Senate. Once a Federation Nation ratifies or rejects an Amendment, the action is final. Any Amendment not ratified within ten years after its submittal to Federation Nations by the Assembly for approval shall be considered rejected.

Chapter VI – Constitutional Supremacy, Establishment and Allegiance

1. All debts contracted before the adoption of this Constitution shall be as valid within the Federation under this Constitution as under the European Union.

2. This Constitution and the laws of the Federation and all treaties and executive agreements which shall be enacted under it, shall be the supreme law of the Federation and the Judges in every Nation shall be bound thereby, anything in a Nation's Constitution or laws to the contrary notwithstanding.

3. The Senators and Delegates of the Federation, National Legislatures of its Member Nations and all executive and judicial officers both of the Federation and of its Member Nations shall be bound by oath or affirmation to support this Constitution, but no religious test shall ever be required as a qualification to any office under the Federation. The Assembly shall determine the wording of the oath but no religious book or symbol shall be required to administer the oath.

4. The rights protected by this Constitution are intended to be the rights of natural Persons. Consequently, the words People, Person, or Citizen as used in this Constitution do not include corporations, limited liability companies, or other corporate entities established by the laws of any Nation, the Federation, or any foreign country. Such corporate entities are subject to such regulation as the People, through their elected National and Federation representatives, deem reasonable and otherwise consistent with the powers of the Assembly and the Nations under this Constitution.

Chapter VII – Ratification and the European Union

The ratification by the People of eighteen Nations of the European Union in separate referendums shall be sufficient for the establishment of this Constitution among the Nations ratifying it. Any Nation that has not ratified this Constitution by the date it is established may only be admitted to the Federation under the provisions of Chapter IV, Article 3 of this Constitution.

The FEN Constitution and its Relation to the US Constitution

Preamble

FEN Constitution Clause:
We, the People of the European Union, in order to: promote peace; maintain freedom, security, and justice; develop and maintain an internal commercial market; sustain economic development; promote social justice and equality; and ensure territorial cohesion and respect for linguistic and cultural diversity, establish this Constitution for the Federation of European Nations.

Related US Constitution Clause:
We the People of the United States, in Order to form a more perfect Union, establish Justice, insure domestic Tranquility, provide for the common defence, promote the general Welfare, and secure the Blessings of Liberty to ourselves and our Posterity, do ordain and establish this Constitution for the United States of America.

Reason for Clause:
The purpose of a preamble is to show a Constitution's origin, scope, and goals. The preamble does not confer any power but only expounds the nature, extent, and application of powers elsewhere in the Constitution.

Impact in the US:
The British colonies in America developed 'The Articles of Confederation' to rule their common interests during the American Revolution. Like the Treaties establishing the European Union, they were insufficient to set up a strong government that would generate the respect of other nations. The Constitutional Convention, set up to amend the Articles, developed a new basis of government.

To the newly free American States, the goal was to establish a stable and energetic government allowing personal liberty. Unlike the Articles which were approved by the State legislatures, delegates chosen by the people met in state conventions to review and approve the US Constitution.

Impact on the European Union:

As the FEN preamble states, the people of the European Union want a new Federation to carry out certain things unable to be obtained under the treaties establishing the European Union. Unlike the treaties setting up the EU, the FEN Constitution is a contract, not among the sovereign nations in Europe, but among the people of Europe. The stated aims are designed to resolve the problems that Europe has experienced before and after the establishment of the EU.

The EU's problems, although not identical, are like the United States' experiences after the American Revolution. As compared with the current EU, the Federation can offer greater protection against external enemies, consistent trade policies, and a European outlook for society, agriculture, commerce, manufacturing, arts, education, and religion. It can also generate larger revenues through taxation and achieve savings due to economies of scale.

Unlike the EU, the Federation will be sovereign in its dealings with other nations. It will represent its members at the UN and will speak for all member nations in international relations. After the Federation becomes active when the Constitution achieves the necessary number of ratifications as spelled out in the FEN Constitution, those entering the Federation will withdraw from the EU under Article 50 of the Consolidated Versions of the Treaty on European Union and the Treaty on the Functioning of the European Union.

Those nations who do not ratify may remain in the remnants of the EU or choose to be independent. It is important the people of the various EU nations approve the Federation Constitution directly so that the authority of the Federation and the authority of the individual National governments come from the same source: the people.

Chapter I – The European Assembly
Article 1 – Legislative Powers

FEN Constitution Clause:
All legislative powers granted herein shall be vested in a European Assembly, which shall consist of two Houses: a Senate and Chamber of Delegates.

Related US Constitution Clause:
All legislative Powers herein granted shall be vested in a Congress of the United States, which shall consist of a Senate and House of Representatives.

Reason for Clause:
At the US Constitutional Convention, two plans were put forward for consideration. The Virginia Plan set up a bicameral legislature whose membership was to be decided by State population. The small States claimed it gave too much power to the larger States. The New Jersey Plan, on the other hand, recommended a unicameral legislature with each State having one vote. A compromise supported a lower house chosen by the people per population and an upper house elected by the State legislatures with each State having equal representation.

Impact on the European Union:
This Chapter describes the structure, methods of election, qualifications of members, authorities, procedures, and limits of the legislative branch of the Federation. Article 1 gives sole legislative power to the Assembly, i.e., the other branches of the Federation (the Executive and the Judiciary) cannot enact laws, nor can the Assembly delegate its powers to the other branches. To legislate properly, the Assembly may ask for information, conduct hearings, and hold investigations.

This clause will replace the four EU institutions that handle legislation with two having full authority to pass laws affecting the entire Federation.

Article 2 – The Chamber of Delegates
Section 1

FEN Constitution Clause:
The Chamber of Delegates shall be composed of Members chosen every four years by the people of each Federation Nation. The People in each Nation shall have the same eligibility in voting for Delegates as they have in voting for the most numerous branch of their Nation's Legislature.

Related US Constitution Clause:
The House of Representatives shall be composed of Members chosen every second Year by the People of the several States, and the Electors in each State shall have the Qualifications requisite for Electors of the most numerous Branch of the State Legislature.

Reason for Clause:
During debate at the Constitutional Convention, discussion focused on the way people could be misled, lending support to those saying State legislatures should choose Representatives to Congress. Opponents argued the legislatures would choose representatives based on their parochial interests rather than the national interest.

On length of terms, some said that the new House should be like the British House of Commons, where the term could not exceed 7 years. Virginia specifically elected its State delegates every 7 years. However, the majority believed in frequent elections binding the representative more closely to his or her constituents. Terms for the House varied in opinion from one to three years, so 2 was taken as the compromise.

As for qualifications, some wanted the States to decide who should qualify for Congress. Others wanted a property ownership requirement.

Impact in the US: Because of the two-year term in the US House, most members spend most of their time raising money for the next election.

Impact on the European Union:
Although current EU Parliament members would have their term of office reduced to four years instead of the current five, the greatest impact on the EU would be the power of the Chamber to initiate legislation, an authority the current EU Parliament does not have.

Section 2

FEN Constitution Clause:
A Delegate must be at least 25 years old at the time of election, have been a Citizen of a Federation Nation for at least 10 years, and must have been a resident of the Nation he or she represents for at least one year prior to the time of election.

Related US Constitution Clause:
No Person shall be a Representative who shall not have attained to the Age of twenty-five Years, and been seven Years a Citizen of the United States, and who shall not, when elected, be an Inhabitant of that State in which he shall be chosen.

Reason for Clause:
During the debate over the US Constitution, some wanted to add a property qualification, an age limit, or a disqualification for indebtedness. Others wanted to leave the qualifications up to the individual States. The age of 25 was decided at the time to be the age of wisdom, experience, and knowledge needed to be a proper representative of the people. Citizenship guaranteed the representative was not subject to a foreign power and residency ensured the representative was familiar with the problems and desires of his or her constituents.

Impact in the US:
A delegate must meet only three requirements to run for election. Congress or a State cannot add to, remove, or change any of them.

Impact on the European Union:
Currently, each EU Nation decides the qualifications of the members it sends to the European Parliament.

Section 3

FEN Constitution Clause:
Each Nation in this Federation shall have a number of Delegates based on its population, excluding non-citizens. A population census shall be made within three years after the first meeting of the European Assembly, and every ten years thereafter, according to rules that the Assembly shall establish by law. The total number of Chamber Delegates shall not exceed 400 but each Nation shall have at least one Delegate. Until the first census takes place, the Nations ratifying this Constitution shall have the following number of Delegates: Austria shall be entitled to elect seven, Belgium nine, Bulgaria six, Cyprus one, Czech Republic eight, Denmark four, Estonia one, Finland four, France fifty-two, Germany sixty-five, Greece nine, Hungary eight, Ireland four, Italy forty-eight, Latvia two, Lithuania three, Luxembourg one, Malta one, Netherlands thirteen, Poland thirty-one, Portugal eight, Romania fifteen, Slovakia four, Slovenia two, Spain thirty-seven, Sweden seven, and the United Kingdom fifty.

Related US Constitution Clause:
Representatives and direct Taxes shall be apportioned among the several States which may be included within this Union, according to their respective Numbers, which shall be determined by adding to the whole Number of free Persons, including those bound to Service for a Term of Years, and excluding Indians not taxed, three fifths of all other Persons. The actual Enumeration shall be made within three Years after the first Meeting of the Congress of the United States, and within every subsequent Term of ten Years, in such Manner as they shall by Law direct. The Number of Representatives shall not exceed one for every thirty Thousand, but each State shall have at Least one Representative; and until such enumeration shall be made, the State of New Hampshire shall be entitled to chuse three, Massachusetts eight, Rhode-Island and Providence Plantations one, Connecticut five, New-York six, New Jersey four, Pennsylvania eight, Delaware one, Maryland six, Virginia ten, North Carolina five, South Carolina five, and Georgia three.

Reason for Clause:
The Constitutional Convention discussed several ways to distribute the representatives among the States. Four options were considered: 1) one vote per state; 2) distribution by property value; 3) distribution by financial contribution; and, 4) distribution by population. The last choice was selected with the slave holding states obtaining extra representation based on the three-fifths of each slave they owned, even though the slaves could not vote. The clause was included despite objections to the three-fifths proposal because the same system was not used to decide representation in the State legislature.

Although the number of representatives was eventually set at 65 in the initial Congress, early proposals in the convention doubled the number, because a larger number would mean less chance of corruption. A smaller number proposal won because it would mean less deliberation.

Some convention delegates favored a census to be conducted annually, but that proved too burdensome. The prohibition against direct taxes was approved to prohibit the Congress from enacting poll taxes (required to vote) or property taxes, both of which were used by the States. A tax on income was not even envisaged at that time.

Impact in the US:
Although the US Constitution clause above is still current, the three-fifths and Indians not taxed issues have been made moot by later Amendments.

Impact on the European Union:
This clause in the FEN Constitution determines the representation in the Chamber of Delegates. The Federation Chamber of Delegates will be limited to 400, less than the 766 now in the European Parliament. The current distribution of seats by degressive proportionality will be replaced by a direct proportionality.

Section 4

FEN Constitution Clause:
When a vacancy occurs in the representation of any Nation in the Chamber, the Head of that Nation's government shall ensure a by-election occurs to fill the vacancy within 30 days.

Related US Constitution Clause:
When vacancies happen in the Representation from any State, the Executive Authority thereof shall issue Writs of Election to fill such Vacancies.

Impact on the European Union:
Under current EU rules, a vacancy in the European Parliament is filled by the party whose representative vacated the position. In the Federation, a special election must be held in the Nation to fill the vacancy ensuring that the chamber delegate is a representative of the people and not the party.

Section 5

FEN Constitution Clause:
The Chamber of Delegates shall choose its Speaker and other officers, and shall have the sole power of impeachment.

Related US Constitution Clause:
The House of Representatives shall chuse their Speaker and other Officers; and shall have the sole Power of Impeachment.

Reason for Clause:
The Speaker does not have to be an elected member of the House. However, all have been.

During the Constitutional Convention, various proposals to remove an abusive executive were put forward. One would have the Congress remove the President upon the request of a majority of State legislatures. Another would have the Congress remove the President at its pleasure similar to a Prime Minister on a no confidence vote.

Impact on the European Union:
The EU elects a President of its Parliament for a term of 2 ½ years, half the term of the Parliament. In the FEN, the Speaker will be elected by the Delegates but will serve at the Chamber's pleasure and can be voted out of the position at any time. The subject of impeachment is absent in the EU treaties.

Article 3 – The European Senate
Section 1

FEN Constitution Clause:
The Senate shall be composed of four Senators from each Nation, elected by the People thereof, for eight years, each Senator having one vote in the Senate. The People in each Nation shall have the same eligibility in voting for Senators as they have in voting for the most numerous branch of their Nation's Legislature.

Related US Constitution Clause:
The Senate of the United States shall be composed of two Senators from each State, elected by the people thereof, for six years; and each Senator shall have one vote. The electors in each State shall have the qualifications requisite for electors of the most numerous branch of the State legislatures.

Reason for Clause: The idea of a bicameral legislature stemmed from the fear of hasty and inappropriate legislation. The Senate provided an impediment in that any law passed had to be approved by the House (People) and then the Senate (States) hopefully ensuring due deliberation and inquiry. When the Senate was brought into the picture as part of a bicameral legislature, it was assumed the Senate would provide a 'Cooling Saucer' for the 'legislative tea' produced by the House.

Several proposals on the structure and election process of the Senate were discussed during the Constitutional Convention. One would have the Senate elected by the House from nominees submitted by the State legislatures. Still another proposal allowed the Executive to appoint Senators from a list submitted by the State legislatures. The idea of State legislatures appointing the Senators was to provide a link between the States and the Federal government. Consequently, the original language of the Constitution gave the power of electing Senators to the State legislatures.

The founding fathers also focused on the number of Senators for each State. A proposal to have them distributed proportionally by population like the House was considered but eventually was discarded in favor of each state having an equal vote. The idea of equal representation was designed to ensure the small states were not overwhelmed by the larger. Two senators also ensured a continuity for the State should one not be reelected.

Impact in the US:
It was changed to a popular vote via Amendment. State legislatures in the late 19th century were corrupted by corporate money to elect Senators that favored corporate rather than national or state interests. Progressive political action enabled an Amendment to the Constitution requiring a popular vote for Senator.

Impact on the European Union:
The upper house of the EU legislature, the Council of the EU, is composed of ministers of the EU nations, depending on the subject. Currently, 10 subject committees can have up to 28 ministers per committee for a total of 280 potential ministers. This unwieldy organization will be replaced with 4 elected Senators per Nation to represent their Nation on all subjects brought before the Assembly.

Section 2

FEN Constitution Clause:
In the first election of Senators, each Nation will assign one of its Senators a term of two years, another four years, another six years and the last the full eight years. In subsequent elections, all Senators will have a term of eight years. The purpose of this procedure is to ensure

that one-quarter of the Senate will face election every two years. When a vacancy occurs in the representation of any Nation in the Senate, the Head of that Nation's government shall ensure a by-election occurs to fill the vacancy within 90 days.

Related US Constitution Clause:
Immediately after they shall be assembled in Consequence of the first Election, they shall be divided as equally as may be into three Classes. The Seats of the Senators of the first Class shall be vacated at the Expiration of the second Year, of the second Class at the Expiration of the fourth Year, and of the third Class at the Expiration of the sixth Year, so that one third may be chosen every second Year; and if Vacancies happen by Resignation, or otherwise, during the Recess of the Legislature of any State, the Executive thereof may make temporary Appointments until the next Meeting of the Legislature, which shall then fill such Vacancies.

Reason for Clause:
At the Constitutional Convention, the delegates, after approving the need for a Senate, discussed the term of office. Some suggested 7 years, others five years and one proposal was to elect Senators for life. The final approved method was for a term of 6 years.   The three-class system was designed to ensure that only 1/3 of the Senate would face election every two years, unlike the entire House which faced election every two years.

The bicameral system reduces the impulse of sudden and violent passions of a House elected every two years. It also provides for continuity of government from one Congressional term to the next. When the first Congress assembled, the Senators chose by lot those who had two year, those with four year, and those with six year terms in accordance with this clause.

The original Constitution gave State legislatures the duty of selecting Senators. If a vacancy occurred, the legislature would elect a replacement or the Governor of the State would choose a temporary replacement until the legislature could assemble.

Impact in the US:
The Seventeenth Amendment revised the procedure by giving the selection to the voters of the State. Now, if a vacancy occurs, a special election is required, but the State legislature in some States may empower the governor to appoint a temporary Senator until the election can be held.

Impact on the European Union:
The Council of the European Union, the upper house of Parliament, is composed of ministers in each Nation's current government. They deal only with issues falling within their expertise. Under the FEN, those politicians and statesmen who would have become prime minister or president of their Nation will now have an opportunity to represent their Nation in a large European entity. Since there will be only four Senators per nation, the degree of power and responsibility to represent the Nation and deal with European issues will be enormous.

Section 3

FEN Constitution Clause:
A Senator must be at least 30 years old at the time of election, have been a Citizen of a Federation Nation for at least 10 years, and must be a resident of the Nation he or she represents for at least one year prior to the time of election.

Related US Constitution Clause:
No Person shall be a *Senator who shall not have attained to the Age of thirty Years, and been nine Years a Citizen of the United States, and who shall not, when elected, be an Inhabitant of that State for which he shall be chosen.*

Reason for Clause:
The age of thirty years was inspired by the age required of a Roman Senator, citizenship was to ensure the Senator was free of foreign influence, and residency was to ensure the Senator had an interest in those things affecting his or her State. During Convention deliberations, one proposal was to require a Senator to have a certain amount of property. Another proposal would have required 14 years of citizenship

over a concern a foreigner would be more loyal to his or her birth country than the US.

Impact in the US:
The US Supreme Court has determined that these qualifications cannot be supplemented or diminished by Congress or by a State.

Impact on the European Union:
In the European Union, the upper house of the European Parliament, is composed of the ministers of each nation. Their qualifications for serving in the upper house are determined by each Nation. No EU wide qualifications exist.

Section 4

FEN Constitution Clause:
The Vice President of the Federation shall be President of the Senate, but shall have no vote, unless it is equally divided. When there is a vacancy in the office of the Vice President, the Vice President is Acting President or unable to serve, the Senate shall appoint a President pro tempore from among its members to preside. The Senate shall choose its other officers.

Related US Constitution Clause:
The Vice President of the United States shall be President of the Senate, but shall have no Vote, unless they be equally divided.

Reason for Clause:
During the Constitutional Convention, some did not see the need for a Vice President. In its original deliberations, the Convention allowed the Senate, like the House, to select its own President/Speaker, who would assume the duties of the Nation's President upon his or her removal, death, resignation or disability. Since that arrangement could create a conflict of interest if there were an impeachment trial, a Vice President was agreed on to assume the Presidency when required, but gave him or her the duty of presiding over the Senate to occupy his or her time.

Impact in the US:
In modern times, the US Vice President only presides over the Senate when a tie vote is anticipated. Even in the absence of the Vice President, the President pro tempore rarely presides over the Senate but appoints junior Senators to preside.

Impact on the European Union:
The current EU has no Vice President. The Council of the European Union (the upper house) has a rotating presidency among the various EU nations.

Section 5

FEN Constitution Clause:
The Senate shall have the sole power to try all impeachments. When the President or Vice President of the Federation is being tried, the Chairman of the European Supreme Court will preside. A vote of two-thirds of Senators present will constitute a conviction and immediate removal from office.

Related US Constitution Clause:
The Senate shall have the sole Power to try all Impeachments. When sitting for that Purpose, they shall be on Oath or Affirmation. When the President of the United States is tried, the Chief Justice shall preside: And no Person shall be convicted without the Concurrence of two thirds of the Members present.

Reason for Clause:
In Great Britain, impeachment resides in the House of Commons and trial in the House of Lords. To the US Founding Fathers, the only body deemed to have the same gravitas to judge another's conduct was the elected Senate. An original unapproved proposal during the Constitutional Convention would have allowed the Congress to remove the President on the request of a majority of the State legislatures. Another proposal made during the Convention would have required the Supreme Court to try impeachments. The reason this proposal was not approved was most delegates considered the Supreme Court to be a

place for legal determinations. Since impeachment is a political rather than a legal action, it should not rest with the judiciary.

However, the Chief Justice of the Supreme Court was added as the president of the court if the President of the US were on trial. The purpose of putting the Chief Justice as the presiding officer at the impeachment trial of the President was to prevent the Vice President, who normally presides over the Senate, from having a conflict of interest in seeing the impeachment succeed.

Another proposal had the only crimes available for impeachment as treason and bribery. Maladministration was later added to the list, but eventually replaced with the phrase 'high crimes and misdemeanors'.

The 75% required for conviction was to prevent party resentment or popular clamor from removing an official whose guilt was not specifically manifest.

Impact in the US:
The US Supreme Court has interpreted the 'sole Power' phrase as giving the Senate the exclusive and unreviewable authority to determine the adequacy of an impeachment trial.

Impact on the European Union:
In the European Union, the President of the European Commission, the Executive arm of the EU, can be removed along with the Commission by a censure vote of the Parliament. If such a situation occurred, there would need to be a bill of censure introduced, a debate on its merits and a simple majority vote to remove the officers.

Section 6

FEN Constitution Clause:
The penalty for an impeachment conviction can only be removal from office and disqualification from further office under the Federation, but the convicted shall still be liable for indictment, trial, judgment, and punishment under law.

Related US Constitution Clause:
Judgment in Cases of impeachment shall not extend further than to removal from Office, and disqualification to hold and enjoy any Office of honor, Trust or Profit under the United States: but the Party convicted shall nevertheless be liable and subject to Indictment, Trial, Judgment and Punishment, according to Law.

Reason for Clause:
The only purpose of an impeachment is to remove an offending public office holder and/or to prevent him or her from ever obtaining an office again, an idea different from British impeachments which might include punishments such as banishment or death. Other authorities may pursue the impeached offender if he or she has broken any law. It was thought that impeachment should only provide a political punishment (removal from office and disqualification from further office), to prevent politicians from using the impeachment process to judicially punish their enemies.

Impact on the European Union:
The EU has no impeachment process.

Article 4 – Elections to the Assembly
Section 1

FEN Constitution Clause:
Each Nation's Legislature shall decide the time, place, and manner of elections to the Chamber and Senate, but the Assembly may, by law, make or change such decisions.

Related US Constitution Clause:
The Times, Places and Manner of holding Elections for Senators and Representatives, shall be prescribed in each State by the Legislature thereof; but the Congress may at any time by Law make or alter such Regulations, except as to the Places of chusing Senators.

Reason for Clause:
In the US, States control voter registration, primary and general elections, place of voting, voting operations, voter protection, fraud prevention, vote counting, duties of poll workers and publication of voting results. States also establish election districts for the House of Representatives. Although Congress does have authority by this clause to override State election procedures, it has done so rarely, most notably by establishing a common general election date and mandating single member districts for House elections. Without such authority, a State could cripple the federal government by refusing to hold an election.

The restriction limiting Congress from determining the places of choosing Senators was to prevent the Congress from mandating the location of the State capital, since Senators were originally selected by State Legislatures. Since senators are now chosen by the people, the clause is moot.

Impact in the US:
Another example was the Voting Rights Act requiring certain jurisdictions to seek approval from the US Attorney General for any voting changes to ensure that certain jurisdictions could not suppress black voting rights. The Supreme Court has also weighed in by requiring each Congressional district to be substantially equal in population.

Impact on the European Union:
In the European Union, the system of election is left to each Nation, but it must be by proportional representation. Under the FEN, the Assembly would have authority to change this.

Section 2

FEN Constitution Clause:
The terms of Senators and Delegates shall end at noon on the 8th day of April of the year the term is to end, when the terms of their successors will begin.

Related US Constitution Clause:
The Congress shall assemble at least once in every Year, and such Meeting shall be on the first Monday in December, unless they shall by Law appoint a different Day. The terms of the President and Vice President shall end at noon on the 20th day of January, and the terms of Senators and Representatives at noon on the 3d day of January, of the years in which such terms would have ended if this article had not been ratified; and the terms of their successors shall then begin.

Reason for Clause:
The US Founding Fathers did not consult their calendars in approving this clause. The original clause (underlined above) required the Congress to meet in December. However, the first term of the new Congress under the Constitution was set as March 4, 1789 by the old Congress under the Articles of Confederation. Therefore, all subsequent terms would begin every other year on March 4 after the recent election.

Impact in the US:
Since the States were responsible for holding elections to Congress, they occurred at various times of the year, some as early as April, until a law mandating a common election day was passed. Because of the requirement to meet in December each year, the old Congress was required to meet on that date in a lame duck session. This error was rectified by the XXnd Amendment (double underlined above) establishing firm dates for terms of Congress and the President.

Impact on the European Union:
The terms of EU Parliament Members begin on the first day that Parliament convenes and ends on the day when the newly elected member takes office.

Section 3

FEN Constitution Clause:
The Assembly shall convene at least once every year beginning at noon on the 8th day of April unless it selects a different day, by law.

Related US Constitution Clause:
The Congress shall assemble at least once in every year, and such meeting shall begin at noon on the 3d day of January, unless they shall by law appoint a different day.

Reason for Clause:
The clause was inserted to ensure Congress met at least annually to discuss national problems of the day. Some naïve delegates at the Constitutional Convention did not think an annual meeting was necessary, once the government was set up and details of commerce and revenue were decided, since they thought the most important legislation would be made at the State level. The majority won out by noting that the British Parliament met every year as a check against the monarchy.

Impact in the US:
Of course, these days, Congress is in session almost year-round.

Impact on the European Union:
The European Parliament meets on the first Tuesday in March each year.

Article 5 – Legislative Procedures
Section 1

FEN Constitution Clause:
Each House shall be the judge of the election and qualifications of its own Members, a majority of which shall constitute a quorum to conduct business. If a quorum does not exist, Members can be compelled to attend in a manner and with penalties as each House may establish.

Related US Constitution Clause:
Each House shall be the Judge of the Elections, Returns and Qualifications of its own Members, and a Majority of each shall constitute a Quorum to do Business; but a smaller Number may adjourn from day to day, and may be authorized to compel the Attendance of

absent Members, in such Manner, and under such Penalties as each House may provide.

Reason for Clause:
It was agreed early in the US Constitutional Convention the legislature must have complete control of the election and qualifications of its members, or its rights and authority could be diluted. The quorum requirement received a lot of attention. A quorum in the British House of Commons was 45 members out of 600.

The first proposal was to imitate the British and prescribe a quorum less than a majority to prevent delay and to stop a few from obstructing business at a critical moment by walking out. On the opposite side, some feared that a small number of representatives could agree to meet early and conduct business beneficial to their States. Still others wanted to leave the decision up to the Congress, by law. Finally, the US Founding Fathers decided on a majority to conduct business to prevent a small number of legislators from hijacking Congress and passing unseemly legislation.

Impact in the US:
Currently, a quorum is assumed in Congress unless a member suggests an absence of one, usually as a delaying tactic.

Impact on the European Union:
In the EU, no standard qualification exists for membership in the parliament. Qualifications are set by and can vary in each Nation. A quorum in the EU parliament exists when one-third of members are present.

Section 2

FEN Constitution Clause:
Each House may determine its own rules of procedure, discipline its Members, and, with the concurrence of two thirds, expel a Member.

Related US Constitution Clause:
Each House may determine the Rules of its Proceedings, punish its Members for disorderly Behaviour, and, with the Concurrence of two thirds, expel a Member.

Reason for Clause:
The requirement for expelling a member on a two thirds vote was not in the original draft developed by the appropriate committee during the Convention, but was introduced in the general session during final approval.

Impact on the European Union:
The EU Parliament develops its own rules and under them Parliament members may be suspended or removed from their offices but cannot be expelled from the Parliament.

Section 3

FEN Constitution Clause:
Each House shall keep a journal of its proceedings and publish it weekly when in session, excluding items that, in its judgment, affect Federation security. The journal shall include the votes of the Members of each House by name on all questions unless a majority of the House present objects.

Related US Constitution Clause:
Each House shall keep a Journal of its Proceedings, and from time to time publish the same, excepting such Parts as may in their Judgment require Secrecy; and the Yeas and Nays of the Members of either House on any question shall, at the Desire of one fifth of those Present, be entered on the Journal.

Reason for Clause:
The ultimate purpose of the section was to ensure legislative transparency. During the Constitutional Convention, some did not want votes on specific issues to be recorded and attributed as a simple tally because some constituents might misinterpret their representative's reasons for his vote. Others did not want the requirement for a journal

in the Constitution because each House would publish one anyway. Although a roll call of votes takes more time than a voice vote, the transparency was eventually determined to be worth it.

Impact on the European Union:
The EU provides an audiovisual record of all Parliament sittings that are available on its Website.

Section 4

FEN Constitution Clause:
Neither House, during an Assembly session, shall adjourn for more than one week, nor to any other place than that in which the two Houses are sitting, without the consent of the other House.

Related US Constitution Clause:
Neither House, during the Session of Congress, shall, without the Consent of the other, adjourn for more than three days, nor to any other Place than that in which the two Houses shall be sitting.

Reason for Clause:
This clause served to eliminate the British system wherein the King or a royal colonial governor could dissolve the legislature and call for new elections. Only the Congress can adjourn itself. The two Houses of Congress cannot meet in different places unless both agree, to ensure a national capital is established and maintained.

Impact in the US:
To overcome the adjournment restriction, at times, the Congress holds pro forma sessions, in which the chamber is called to order and promptly recessed every three days without an actual adjournment.

Impact on the European Union:
In the EU, Parliament makes the rules for its adjournment. EU Sessions locations are established in the underlying treaties establishing the EU.

Article 6 – Compensation, Privileges, and Restrictions
Section 1

FEN Constitution Clause:
Senators and Delegates shall receive compensation for their services from the Federation Treasury according to law. They cannot be arrested or detained while en route to or from a session of their respective Houses, except for treason or felony. Any speech or debate occurring during a House session shall not be questioned in any other place.

Related US Constitution Clause:
The Senators and Representatives shall receive a Compensation for their Services, to be ascertained by Law, and paid out of the Treasury of the United States. They shall in all Cases, except Treason, Felony and Breach of the Peace, be privileged from Arrest during their Attendance at the Session of their respective Houses, and in going to and returning from the same; and for any Speech or Debate in either House, they shall not be questioned in any other Place.

Reason for Clause:
This clause was a major point of debate during the Convention. The delegates realized there were persons of talent lacking independent means who could not run for election or would be tempted to corruption, without some compensation. Some delegates wanted Congressional salaries to be paid by their respective State legislatures, while others wanted salaries to be fixed to the price of a commodity, like wheat.

Objections were raised that a State legislature could force the resignation of an elected representative they did not agree with by reducing or eliminating his salary. Another option proposed derived from certain colonial legislatures who paid their representatives through a tax on their constituents. The final clause language agreed to allowed compensation to be determined by the Congress itself, although the first Congress under the Constitution restricted this privilege (See Article 6, Section 3.)

The second part of the clause, the privilege of non-arrest, was a familiar rule in both British and colonial law. The purpose was to prevent the King or his Royal Governor Executive from arresting a Member of Parliament to prevent his voting on an issue.

Similarly, the free speech privilege was enshrined in British and colonial law, immunizing representatives from libel or slander suits.

Impact in the US:
The Supreme Court has ruled the free speech privilege applies also to Congressional staff in support of their Congressman or Senator. However, it does not apply to any speeches made off the floor of Congress or if published by the speechmaker.

Impact on the European Union:
In the EU, a Parliament member's salary is formula driven. A member of the EU Parliament has the same immunities in his own Nation as a member of his National Legislature has plus he is immune from arrest in other EU Nations unless caught in a criminal act. He is also protected from statements made as part of his official duties.

Section 2

FEN Constitution Clause:
Senators and Delegates, during their terms of election, shall not accept or serve in any civil office of the Federation. A Person serving in any civil office of the Federation must resign that position before standing for election to the Assembly.

Related US Constitution Clause:
No Senator or Representative shall, during the Time for which he was elected, be appointed to any civil Office under the Authority of the United States, which shall have been created, or the Emoluments whereof shall have been encreased during such time; and no Person holding any Office under the United States, shall be a Member of either House during his Continuance in Office.

Reason for Clause:
The clause exists not only to protect the separation of powers between the legislature and executive but also to prevent Congress from establishing offices to which members of Congress would be appointed. It also prevents the President from using his appointment authority to buy votes in Congress in return for a Presidential appointment. The clause also closes the possibility of a parliamentary system of government emerging in which members of Congress hold cabinet posts.

The clause does not prevent a federal judge from serving in the Executive Branch.

Impact on the European Union:
The EU Parliament Rules of Procedure does not prohibit a Member from simultaneously serving in another office of the European Union.

Section 3

FEN Constitution Clause:
No law varying the compensation for the services of the Senators and Delegates shall take effect until an election of Delegates shall have intervened.

Related US Constitution Clause:
No law varying the compensation for the services of the Senators and Representatives shall take effect until an election of Representatives shall have intervened.

Reason for Clause:
This clause was not in the original Constitution but was added later as an amendment, proposed by the first Congress in 1789. However, it was not fully approved by the required number of States until 1992. The idea was to prohibit the Congress from too freely increasing its salaries.

Impact in the US:
The courts have ruled this clause does not apply to automatic cost of living increases.

Impact on the European Union:
In the EU, the salary of members of parliament is set at 38.5% of the salary of a European Court of Justice Judge. The Judges' salary is based on the secret Brussels International index.

Article 7 – Legislative Bills
Section 1

FEN Constitution Clause:
All bills for raising revenue shall originate in the Chamber of Delegates. The Senate may agree to, or decrease the amount of revenue in a bill but shall not increase the amount or add revenue by amending another bill. Other bills from the Chamber can be amended or concurred with by the Senate. The Senate may initiate bills that do not raise revenue.

Related US Constitution Clause:
All Bills for raising Revenue shall originate in the House of Representatives; but the Senate may propose or concur with Amendments as on other Bills.

Reason for Clause:
Unlike the EU, a bill in the US Congress can be introduced in either the House or the Senate, except for tax bills. The idea came from the British system where the House of Commons had the first reading of a revenue bill. The House of Lords could not alter a tax bill passed by the Commons, but could only accept or reject it. The US Constitution, however, does allow the Senate to amend tax bills passed by the House. Some at the convention did not see a problem with tax bills originating in the Senate, since the Senate was not a House of Lords, unrepresentative of the people.

Impact in the US:
In practice, the US Senate has overcome the restrictions of this clause by placing tax language in a non-revenue bill passed by the House. However, the FEN language eliminates that option.

Impact on the European Union:
In the EU, the Parliament has no power to tax, but can provide its opinion on tax legislation. The taxing power remains with the EU national governments.

Section 2

FEN Constitution Clause:
Every bill that passes the Chamber of Delegates and the Senate shall be provided to the President of the Federation. If the President approves it, he or she shall sign it and it will become law. If the President does not approve it, it will be returned to the House it originated from, along with the President's reasons for disapproval. The House will enter the President's reasons into its journal and reconsider the bill. If, after reconsideration, two thirds of the House agree to pass the bill, it will be sent to the other House along with the President's reasons for disapproval. The other House will proceed in a like manner to reconsider the bill and if passed by two thirds of that House, it shall become law. In such cases, all votes shall be recorded in the journal of each House and the names of the Members voting for and against the bill shall be recorded. If a bill is not returned by the President to the Assembly within 10 days after submittal to him or her, it shall become law, unless the Assembly has prevented its return by adjournment.

Related US Constitution Clause:
Every Bill which shall have passed the House of Representatives and the Senate, shall, before it become a Law, be presented to the President of the United States; If he approve he shall sign it, but if not he shall return it, with his Objections to that House in which it shall have originated, who shall enter the Objections at large on their Journal, and proceed to reconsider it. If after such Reconsideration two thirds of that House shall agree to pass the Bill, it shall be sent, together with the Objections, to the other House, by which it shall likewise be reconsidered, and if approved by two thirds of that House, it shall become a Law. But in all such Cases the Votes of both Houses shall be determined by yeas and Nays, and the Names of the Persons voting for and against the Bill shall be entered on the Journal of each House respectively. If any Bill shall not be returned by the President within ten Days (Sundays excepted) after it

shall have been presented to him, the Same shall be a Law, in like Manner as if he had signed it, unless the Congress by their Adjournment prevent its Return, in which Case it shall not be a Law.

Reason for Clause:
This clause is the veto clause, even though the word is not mentioned. It gives the President the power to halt legislation by refusing to sign it and sending it back to the House from whence it came with his written objections. If two thirds of both Houses repass the bill, it becomes law without the President's signature. In any case, if the President does not return it to Congress signed or unsigned within 10 days, it also becomes law.

During Constitutional debate, it was noted the King of Great Britain could veto any act of Parliament with no recourse. At the Constitutional Convention, there was clear opposition to the Executive having the same veto power. Consequently, the principal points discussed during the Convention were how the veto should be qualified, by what number of each House was needed to overturn the veto, and whether the veto should be shared by the president with another body.

Some were concerned that giving the Executive the veto was in effect establishing an elective monarchy. One alternative proposed was to allow the Executive to suspend an act of Congress for a specific period. Another option floated was to allow the Judiciary to be involved in the review of laws, to avoid passage of a bad law. That idea was dismissed after it was pointed out that the Court's opinion might be influenced by its previous decisions on the subject.

Discussion over the proper number of Congressional members needed to overturn a Presidential veto centered on either 2/3 or 3/4.

Impact on the European Union:
Looking at the simplicity of this article and this clause on how legislation is to be handled in the US Constitution, the procedure in the EU is byzantine. Legislation in the EU can follow either the ordinary procedure or four special procedures, depending upon the content of the bill proposed. The process must start with the Commission because

only the Commission may propose legislation. The ordinary procedure is the usual process through which directives and regulations are adopted:

1. The Commission provides a legislative proposal to the Parliament and Council.
2. At the first reading, Parliament amends or accepts the language of the proposal.
3. If the Parliament accepts the language, the proposal becomes law.
4. If the Parliament amends the proposal and the Council approves Parliament's revised wording, then the proposal becomes law.
5. If not, the Council must amend the language and pass it back to Parliament with reasons for the change.
6. At the second reading, if the Parliament approves the Council's wording, the proposal becomes law.
7. If it does not, the Parliament may amend the new language it and pass it back to the Council.
8. If the Council approves the new wording, it becomes law.
9. If after 3 months, the Council has not approved the new wording, the Council President must convene a Conciliation committee to draw up a joint proposal.
10. If a joint proposal is not agreed upon in six weeks, the proposal is void.
11. If a joint proposal is agreed upon, then the Council and Parliament must approve the language at third reading.
12. If either fails to approve the proposal text, the law is void.

Besides this, there are four special procedures used for sensitive or specific cases:

- Consultation Procedure - normally used for legislation on internal market exemptions and competition law: the Council can adopt legislation based on a proposal by the Commission after consulting Parliament.

- Consent Procedure – used to admit new members to the Union, produce methods of withdrawal or to combat discrimination:
    1. The Council adopts a law after obtaining Parliament consent.

2. The Parliament may not propose amendments.

- Commission and Council acting alone – used when setting common external tariff and trade agreements: the Council can adopt legislation without Parliament.

- Commission acting alone – used for legislation on monopolies and concessions granted to companies by Member Nations, and on rights of workers to remain in a Member State.

Section 3

FEN Constitution Clause:
All orders, resolutions, or votes that require the concurrence of the Senate and Chamber of Delegates, except for adjournment or amendments to this Constitution, shall be provided to the President of the Federation for approval before they can take effect. If such orders, resolutions, or votes are not approved, they may be repassed by a vote of two thirds of the Senate and Chamber of Delegates according to the same rules prescribed for a bill.

Related US Constitution Clause:
Every Order, Resolution, or Vote to which the Concurrence of the Senate and House of Representatives may be necessary (except on a question of Adjournment) shall be presented to the President of the United States; and before the Same shall take Effect, shall be approved by him, or being disapproved by him, shall be repassed by two thirds of the Senate and House of Representatives, according to the Rules and Limitations prescribed in the Case of a Bill.

Reason for Clause:
This section applies the procedures of the Presentment clause (previous section) to all Assembly business requiring the consent of both Houses. The only exceptions are adjournments and constitutional amendments. It was added to prevent the Congress from usurping the President's authority in approving laws by calling them something else.

Article 8 – Legislative Powers

FEN Constitution Clause:
The Assembly shall have power:

Related US Constitution Clause:
The Congress shall have Power

Reason for Clause:
This article introduces the enumerated powers of the Congress.

Impact in the US:
The US Courts have broadly interpreted these enumerated powers.

Impact on the European Union:
In the European Union, the Parliament has authority to approve but not initiate legislation. Even this authority is limited as Laws passed by the Parliament may be delayed by National Legislatures.

Section 1

FEN Constitution Clause:
To impose and collect taxes, import duties, and excises and pay the debts and fund the common defense and general welfare of the Federation, but all import duties, and excises shall be uniform throughout the Federation;

Related US Constitution Clause:
The Congress shall have Power To lay and collect Taxes, Duties, Imposts and Excises, to pay the Debts and provide for the common Defence and general Welfare of the United States; but all Duties, Imposts and Excises shall be uniform throughout the United States;

Reason for Clause:
Every government needs authority to support its military forces, pay its employees and its debts from a national treasury. Consequently, the power to obtain money is an essential power of government. One of the main defects of the Articles of Confederation was the Confederation

Congress's lack of authority to tax. To fund the workings of the new nation, requests for funds were made to the States which could pay all of them, part of them, or none of them. Therefore, this clause was very important to the delegates at the Constitutional Convention to independently fund the operations of the new federal government.

Impact in the US:
In many cases, however, revenue has not been the only motive behind taxation. Congress has used taxation to regulate commerce, discourage commerce and protect native industries. The power of taxation granted in this clause is limited by other parts of the Constitution, i.e., where tax bills may be introduced (only the House of Representatives); no export taxes allowed; and all spending authorized in law.

The phrase 'fund the common defense and general welfare of the United States' has been interpreted in two ways. One group, strict constructionists, claims the phrase is an introduction to the following clauses and has little meaning. Loose constructionists claim the phrase is in addition to the powers that follow.

The Supreme Court ruled in 1796 that the federal government has the authority to tax anything except exports.

Impact on the European Union:
Of note: The European Union has no taxing powers.

Section 2

FEN Constitution Clause:
To borrow money on the credit of the Federation, the validity of which, as authorized by law, shall not be questioned;

Related US Constitution Clause:
To borrow Money on the credit of the United States;

The validity of the public debt of the United States, authorized by law, including debts incurred for payment of pensions and bounties for services in suppressing insurrection or rebellion, shall not be questioned.

But neither the United States nor any State shall assume or pay any debt or obligation incurred in aid of insurrection or rebellion against the United States, or any claim for the loss or emancipation of any slave; but all such debts, obligations and claims shall be held illegal and void.

Reason for Clause:
A right that was granted to the Congress under the Articles of Confederation was deemed a right of every sovereign government.

Impact on the European Union:
The EU has no authority to issue bonds or assume debt, which should say something about its sovereignty.

Section 3

FEN Constitution Clause:
To regulate commerce with foreign countries and among the Nations of the Federation;

Related US Constitution Clause:
To regulate Commerce with foreign Nations, and among the several States, and with the Indian Tribes;

Reason for Clause:
The Articles of Confederation provided no authority to the central government to regulate commerce. However, the Articles did give Congress authority over trade and other affairs involving Indians, if the Indians were not residents of a State. At the Constitutional Convention, this clause received much attention in committee action. Commercial interests at the time were regionally based and wanted these interests protected: fisheries, West Indies trade, shipping, wheat, tobacco, rice and indigo.

Some delegates wanted any law regulating commerce to require the approval of two thirds of each house. The northern States wanted preference given to American ships and wanted a strong navy. The southern States did not want to have any federal regulation of commerce, because they feared the northern states would raise shipping rates if only American ships were required for trade.

Impact in the US:
During the first 100 years of the Constitution's existence, the clause was used by the Supreme Court to prohibit State legislation granting monopolies. After that period, the clause was used to prohibit monopolistic practices by corporations.

Early on, the Supreme Court, under this clause, ruled the federal government had control over all navigable waters (being a method of interstate transport) in the US. The Court also designated American Indian Tribes as not being equal to other sovereign nations, describing them in relation to the US as a ward to a guardian. Consequently, the federal government can regulate trade with the Indian Tribes within or outside State boundaries.

A landmark Supreme Court decision confirmed the authority of the federal government to regulate interstate commerce and its supremacy over State law by declaring a State law invalid that prohibited oystering by non-State residents. The court also prohibited a State from requiring an import license to bring in goods. But, the Supreme Court did permit a State to enact a commerce law in an area the federal government did not regulate.

Although the definition of commerce was originally limited to the concept of trade, it has since been expanded to mean industrial production, agriculture, mining, etc. The current interpretation is that Congress may regulate: 1) the channels of interstate commerce; 2) the instruments, persons or things of interstate commerce even though they arise from intrastate activities; and, 3) activities having a substantial relation to interstate commerce.

Under this meaning, the Supreme Court has validated Civil Rights legislation.

Impact on the European Union:
Although the original purpose of the EU was to establish a single market for its members, all phases of this objective have not been implemented. Not all its members accept the free movement of people into their jurisdiction, nor do all use the same currency. And notably, member nations still attend international economic and trade conferences representing their own nations.

Section 4

FEN Constitution Clause:
To establish uniform laws of Citizenship, immigration, naturalization, and bankruptcies throughout the Federation;

Related US Constitution Clause:
To establish an uniform Rule of Naturalization, and uniform Laws on the subject of Bankruptcies throughout the United States;

All persons born or naturalized in the United States, and subject to the jurisdiction thereof, are citizens of the United States and of the State wherein they reside.

Reason for Clause:
Under the Articles of Confederation, each State designated its citizens, but also had to respect the citizenship decisions of the other States, causing much confusion. Prior to the 14th Amendment to the Constitution, the States set the standards for citizenship, even though the Constitution gave this right to the Congress.

The bankruptcy clause was added late in the Constitutional Convention as some delegates noted bankruptcy laws in the States tended to benefit the State rather than the national interest. Since a creditor may have many financial interests and properties in various States, each State would apply its own laws to the issue diminishing a thriving commerce that the founding fathers intended to create. Similarly, other nations would become frustrated having to deal with each State's bankruptcy laws.

Impact in the US:
The courts have since established the federal government is the only source of bankruptcy law in the US.

Impact on the European Union:
Note that every citizen of an EU member State is a citizen of the EU. And although each Nation handles bankruptcies per its own laws, EU regulations require the laws of the nation where the bankrupt party's assets are most centered to be used to determine disposition of the assets.

Section 5

FEN Constitution Clause:
To produce Federation coin and currency, to regulate their value and that of foreign currency, and to establish the Federation standard of weights and measures;

Related US Constitution Clause:
To coin Money, regulate the Value thereof, and of foreign Coin, and fix the Standard of Weights and Measures;

Reason for Clause:
The original Articles of Confederation gave the minting of coin to the Congress but left the valuing of foreign coin unaddressed.

Impact in the US:
Prior to the Civil War, the federal government issued coin but not paper currency. The States chartered banks which issued bank notes used as currency but whose values fluctuated depending on the bank of issuance and general economic conditions. This system caused frequent bank panics and depressions and inhibited interstate commerce until the US began issuing paper currency backed by the credit of the US during the Civil War.

Impact on the European Union:
The EU is held together by the Euro, the common currency issued by the European Central Bank, one of the independent institutions established

under the treaties that created the EU. However, not all EU members have the Euro as their currency.

Section 6

FEN Constitution Clause:
To prescribe measures to prevent counterfeiting of the securities, coin and currency of the Federation;

Related US Constitution Clause:
To provide for the Punishment of counterfeiting the Securities and current Coin of the United States;

Reason for Clause:
During the Constitutional Convention, the group deemed the federal government would be in the best position to control and punish counterfeiters.

Impact in the US:
Since then, Courts have decided that the States and the federal government have concurrent power to enforce counterfeiting laws. The federal government can punish counterfeiting because it affects the integrity of the federal financial system. The States may punish passing of counterfeit currency or securities because it defrauds State citizens.

Impact on the European Union:
The EU has laws against Euro counterfeiting. However, the identification of and punishment for counterfeit currency and coin is left in the hands of individual EU nations.

Section 7

FEN Constitution Clause:
To establish and maintain a postal service;

Related US Constitution Clause:
To establish Post Offices and post Roads;

Reason for Clause:
The problems delivering mail among the colonies with 13 separate mail policies led to the idea the national government should manage a national postal system. Maintaining communication among the new States of the US was also seen as a method of strengthening the union and encouraging trade. During the Convention, establishing post roads was accepted, but a motion to include the authority to cut canals where necessary was defeated.

Impact in the US:
The Congress, thirty years later, designated all navigable waters as post roads. Although the word 'establish' in the clause seems to give Congress the authority to erect, make, form, regulate and preserve post roads, Congress did not use the power to construct post roads but only to designate existing roads as post roads.

Impact on the European Union:
The EU has a Postal Directive that establishes the basic minimum of services to be provided by each nation to promote a single postal market.

Section 8

FEN Constitution Clause:
To promote innovation and research by establishing laws for copyrights, patents, trademarks, and other intellectual property;

Related US Constitution Clause:
To promote the Progress of Science and useful Arts, by securing for limited Times to Authors and Inventors the exclusive Right to their respective Writings and Discoveries;

Reason for Clause:
Now known as the Intellectual Property Clause of the US Constitution, the delegates to the Constitutional Convention agreed the States could not deal with this on a State by State basis as it would cause too much confusion and litigation. Consequently, several proposals were made during the Convention that were winnowed into this clause. Examples

included: to secure to authors copy rights for a limited time; to establish a university; to encourage by payment the advancement of useful knowledge; to establish seminaries for promotion of the arts and sciences; to grant corporate charters; to grant patents; and to establish public institutions and rewards for promotion of agriculture, commerce, trade and manufacturing.

These were distilled into three phrases. One would 'secure to authors exclusive rights for a limited time.' The second would 'secure to literary authors their copyrights for a limited time', while the third was 'to encourage, by proper premiums and Provisions, the advancement of useful knowledge and discoveries." The clause as written provides the basis for US copyright law and US patent law. The clause does not protect trademarks but they are protected under the Commerce Clause.

Impact in the US:
The language of the 18th century has changed meaning. 'Useful arts' encompasses not only painters and sculptors but the work of those skilled in manufacturing. 'Science' refers to all knowledge not just those areas subject to the scientific method. In applying this clause, the courts have determined writings are protected only if original and inventions must be inventive and not just improvements on current ideas.

Impact on the European Union:
The EU has two bodies that handle intellectual property. The Office for Harmonization in the Internal Market provides rules for registration of Community trademarks and designs. The European Patent Office is the place where the European Commission is trying to implement a Community patent system.

Section 9

FEN Constitution Clause:
To define and punish piracies, crimes committed in international waters, and violations of international law;

Related US Constitution Clause:
To define and punish Piracies and Felonies committed on the high Seas, and Offences against the Law of Nations;

Reason for Clause:
This clause was assumed to be a function of the national government at the Constitutional Convention as a State with this power might embroil the entire country in a dispute or war.

Impact on the European Union:
On the other hand, EU member nations have complete authority on interpretation of international law. Although the EU can sponsor joint activity among its members, interests of the member Nations on international issues can be conflicting.

Section 10

FEN Constitution Clause:
To authorize and limit the use of military force and establish rules concerning prisoners of war and captured property;

Related US Constitution Clause:
To declare War, grant Letters of Marque and Reprisal, and make Rules concerning Captures on Land and Water;

Reason for Clause:
The need for this clause was to remedy a defect in the Articles of Confederation. Congress, under the Articles, could not prevent or support a war, punish treaty violations or piracy. In fact, under those Articles, a State could provoke a war with a foreign nation, since the only military forces were the State militias. During debate over the Constitution, it was suggested a declaration of war should be approved only in the Senate as it was the more experienced group that would be less likely to act rashly. Others believed war exacted a large burden on the people, and therefore the House should also be part of the decision, particularly since revenue needed for the conflict would have to begin in the House.

Impact in the US:
The phrase 'declare war' in the US Constitution is controversial. The courts have stated that Congress can authorize a state of war by providing funds or authorizing military action even though the word 'declare' or 'declaration' is not present. The President's authority to take military action is confusing, modified by various Congressional acts and international treaties. The phrase 'letters of marque and reprisal' is an anachronism because such instruments are prohibited by international treaties.

Although Congress originally established Prize Courts to dispose of assets seized in war, the US District Courts now have that authority. However, since the last prize court was convened in 1956, the concept is also an anachronism.

Impact on the European Union:
Because the EU is an economic and not a military union, the EU on its own has no power to declare war, initiate conflict or invade a non-EU nation. However, through NATO, some of its members can participate in peacekeeping or anti-terrorist actions.

Section 11

FEN Constitution Clause:
To create and support a Federation Armed Force for defense of the Federation and its Nations;

Related US Constitution Clause:
To raise and support Armies, but no Appropriation of Money to that Use shall be for a longer Term than two Years;
To provide and maintain a Navy;

Reason for Clause:
This clause provided distinct power to Congress to raise an army even though the US founders felt a standing army was a threat to freedom. Some wanted to amend the language to limit the number of troops raised. Others wanted an appropriation no longer than one year. A navy, on the other hand, was not conceived as a threat to freedom.

The delegates compared their situation with that of Great Britain. Because Great Britain was on an island, a large standing army was unneeded as it maintained its security with a strong navy, preventing a foreign invasion force. Many considered the US in the same situation, since the only strong nations were far across the Atlantic and their nearest colonies were not dangerous. However, others argued an emergency was impossible to foresee and any limits would prove dangerous. In fact, they overlooked the threats that faced the new nation. British Canada and its forts in the northwest posed a direct threat as well as the hostile Indian tribes outside the boundaries of the country. Without a standing army of some size and extensive fortifications, these threats could not be countered.

The American Revolution proved State militia were useless in the heat of battle and a part time militia would not be practicable to man fortifications for any length of time. The language of the clause resolved the contradiction.

Impact on the European Union:
Note that the EU has a Common Security and Defense Policy although each member nation maintains its own military force. Twenty-one of the 28 EU members are members of NATO, a military alliance including non-EU members the US, Turkey and Canada.

Section 12

FEN Constitution Clause:
To make rules for managing the Federation Armed Force;

Related US Constitution Clause:
To make Rules for the Government and Regulation of the land and naval Forces;

Reason for Clause:
Although this clause was not in the original draft of the Constitution, it was added because it was in the Articles of Confederation. The British King had this authority but the delegates thought it more appropriate to place this power under the Congress rather than the President. The

sentiment against a standing army that pervaded the Convention caused some to suggest modifying the clause to say the Army would not exceed one thousand men in peacetime.

More logical heads argued that such a clause would only allow raising an army when the country was attacked and not allow for preparation against a threat. The final clause put the trust in Congress to protect the country and at the same time prevent the oppression of its people.

Impact in the US:
This clause has resulted in the Universal Code of Military Justice, the foundation of military law in the US.

Impact on the European Union:
Although there is a European Defence Agency supporting member nations in achieving their targets defined in the Common Security and Defence Policy, each member nation sets its own military budgets, policies and plans. That may change as the European Assembly directs.

Section 13

FEN Constitution Clause:
To provide rules for summoning the Armed Forces of Federation Nations to execute the laws of the Federation, suppress insurrections, and repel invasions;

Related US Constitution Clause:
To provide for calling forth the Militia to execute the Laws of the Union, suppress Insurrections and repel Invasions;

Reason for Clause:
To defend the nation, the delegates were faced with a choice: a standing professional army or citizen militias. The Convention favored militias despite their poor record of service during the American Revolution.

Impact in the US:
Fearing a President using a standing army to oppress the people, Congress passed the Insurrection Act in 1807 to limit the President's authority to suppress insurrections, giving that power to State and local governments. Later the Posse Comitatus Act prevented the President from using the military to enforce laws unless specifically authorized by Congress.

Impact on the European Union:
One can equate the armed forces of each Member Nation of the EU with the State militias, but the comparison has its limits. Obviously, the military capabilities of the EU member nations differ markedly. Under this clause, the Assembly has authority to determine when, where and how a Member Nation's armed forces can be used. This clause may be one of the most difficult ones for a Member Nation with a strong military tradition to accept.

Section 14

FEN Constitution Clause:
To provide rules for organizing, arming, and disciplining the Armed Forces of Federation Nations and for governing them when in the service of the Federation, reserving to each Nation the appointment of officers, and training of its Armed Forces according to the discipline prescribed by the European Assembly;

Related US Constitution Clause:
To provide for organizing, arming, and disciplining, the Militia, and for governing such Part of them as may be employed in the Service of the United States, reserving to the States respectively, the Appointment of the Officers, and the Authority of training the Militia according to the discipline prescribed by Congress;

Reason for Clause:
The purpose of the clause was to ensure uniformity of State militias throughout the US. At the Constitutional Convention, there were objections to this clause. Some argued that the States would never submit to national rules governing their militias. Truthfully, some States

neglected their militias. Those delegates with military experience knew the States would not keep a proper discipline over their militias without the national government keeping the pressure on.

Still others were concerned that Congress could refuse to arm or organize the State militia, leaving the State defenseless. That idea was dismissed, saying that the State could certainly equip its militia should Congress refuse to act.

Impact in the US:
The Supreme Court has stated the President, acting under Congressional authorization, has exclusive and unreviewable authority to call out militia without interference of any State.

Impact on the European Union:
This clause will allow the European Assembly to determine when, where, and how the Armed Forces of its member nations will be used.

Section 15

FEN Constitution Clause:
To exercise legislative authority in all cases over the seat of government, not to exceed five contiguous square miles, within which no Person shall take up residence, that is ceded by a Nation and accepted by the European Assembly;

Related US Constitution Clause:
To exercise exclusive Legislation in all Cases whatsoever, over such District (not exceeding ten Miles square) as may, by Cession of particular States, and the Acceptance of Congress, become the Seat of the Government of the United States, and to exercise like Authority over all Places purchased by the Consent of the Legislature of the State in which the Same shall be, for the Erection of Forts, Magazines, Arsenals, dock-Yards, and other needful Buildings;--And

Reason for Clause:
During the Convention, some delegates wanted to eliminate from consideration as the national capital cities where a state capitol existed

as it would confuse federal/state jurisdictions. Delegates from Pennsylvania and New York objected since both Philadelphia and New York City (state capitals at the time) had hopes of becoming the national capital. Other delegates wanted to select a place and name it in the Constitution. Still others wanted the clause to require the first Congress to select a site.

The idea that the federal government would have complete control over its capital did not cause concern. Without this authority, a State might hinder federal authority, violate its records and cause the federal government to rely on the State for its protection.

Impact in the US:
The District of Columbia, the US federal district, has given Congress unique constitutional problems since it is not a State but it does have residents as any normal city would have. Early on, the Supreme Court declared a resident of the federal district could not sue a citizen of a State in federal court, since the District was not a State and therefore, the courts had no jurisdiction. Similarly, the Supreme Court decided that it could not hear appeals from the federal court Congress had established in the federal District on the same grounds. Congress fixed both problems.

Congress has also given the District its own government, a mayor and council elected by District residents. Congress still has exclusive jurisdiction, however, and can change the city government at any time and even assume direct control of the District. The residents do not have representation in Congress since the District is not a State. However, the residents can vote for President because of a Constitutional Amendment that allows the district 3 electoral votes.

Impact on the European Union:
These problems will be moot for the FEN since its capital will have no residents. Only public buildings and businesses will be permitted. The seven institutions of the EU are spread across four cities: Brussels, Luxembourg, Strasbourg and Frankfurt, although Brussels is referred to as the EU capital.

Section 16

FEN Constitution Clause:
To limit, regulate, and prohibit the labor of Persons less than eighteen years of age;

Related US Constitution Clause:
Not addressed in the US Constitution

Reason for Clause:
This issue was never addressed at the Constitutional Convention mainly because industrialization had not yet occurred and most children who did work did so on family farms.

Impact in the US:
Abuses that occurred in the late 19th century textile mills and mines led for a call for federal action. However, attempts in the late 19th and early 20th century by Congress to address the child labor issue were squelched by the conservative Supreme Court declaring laws prohibiting child labor or taxing companies that employed children as unconstitutional. The Court said the federal government had no power to regulate labor conditions.

Congress passed a child labor amendment to the Constitution in 1924 allowing the federal government to regulate or prohibit child labor and submitted it to the States for approval but the required number never approved it. However, the push for this amendment ended when Congress passed the Fair Labor Standards Act in 1938, regulating the employment of persons under the age of 16. Curiously, a unanimous Supreme Court ruled that act constitutional.

Impact on the European Union:
In the EU, any EU directive must be incorporated into each member Nation's laws. However, it is up to the Member Nation to enforce those laws. An EU Directive prohibits those under 15 from working. However, each member Nation must enforce that law. Under the FEN Constitution, the FEN will have authority to set up enforcement procedures to implement any laws the Assembly passes.

Section 17

FEN Constitution Clause:
To exercise exclusive legislative authority in all cases over real property acquired for the needs of the Federation with the consent of the affected Nation's Legislature; and,

Related US Constitution Clause:
To exercise exclusive Legislation in all Cases whatsoever, over such District (not exceeding ten Miles square) as may, by Cession of particular States, and the Acceptance of Congress, become the Seat of the Government of the United States, and to exercise like Authority over all Places purchased by the Consent of the Legislature of the State in which the Same shall be, for the Erection of Forts, Magazines, Arsenals, dock-Yards, and other needful Buildings;--And

Reason for Clause:
Although this power is provided to every State legislature, some at the Constitutional Convention feared that the federal government would purchase large amounts of land in a State to exert undue influence. The phrase requiring the approval of the affected State's legislature overcame this objection. Others were concerned that such property could house a standing army to be used to threaten a State or even serve as a refuge for State fugitives.

Impact in the US:
In any case, such concerns have not happened even though the Courts have determined State law has no effect on federal property in the State.

Impact on the European Union:
The policy in the EU is stronger than this clause as the EU's property shall be inviolable and exempt from search, requisition, confiscation or expropriation by any Member Nation. There also appears to be no restriction on purchasing real property in any Member Nation by the EU.

Section 18

FEN Constitution Clause:
To legislate where necessary and proper to execute the foregoing powers and all other powers provided in this Constitution to the government of the Federation, its offices or officers.

Related US Constitution Clause:
To make all Laws which shall be necessary and proper for carrying into Execution the foregoing Powers, and all other Powers vested by this Constitution in the Government of the United States, or in any Department or Officer thereof.

Reason for Clause:
Although this clause appears to have generated little controversy at the Convention, there was tremendous objection to it after its submittal to the States. The potential for a tyrannous Congress to overwhelm State authority was voiced. Its proponents countered that the clause only gave Congress the power to make laws. Some questioned who would judge whether a law was necessary or proper. What may be necessary today may be unnecessary tomorrow.

Its proponents said whether a law was necessary was up to Congress and whether it was proper was up to the voters at the next election.

Impact in the US:
In the landmark case McCulloch vs Maryland, the Supreme Court determined the Constitution gave the federal government 'implied' powers to implement the 'expressed' powers. The current interpretation assumes that if the purpose of a Congressional Act is constitutional, the method chosen to implement it is also constitutional.

Impact on the European Union:
In the EU, on the other hand, there is no limit to what the Assembly may legislate.

Article 9 – Limits on the European Assembly
Section 1

FEN Constitution Clause:
An order requiring a Person under arrest to be brought before a judge, known otherwise as a writ of habeas corpus, shall not be suspended unless the safety of the public requires it in the case of rebellion or invasion.

Related US Constitution Clause:
The Privilege of the Writ of Habeas Corpus shall not be suspended, unless when in Cases of Rebellion or Invasion the public Safety may require it.

Reason for Clause:
A writ of habeas corpus is a legal action commanding a law enforcement or other government agency to bring forth a person held in custody for inquiry into the legality of his/her detention. This privilege was enshrined in British Common Law. Such privileges can be suspended in case of invasion or rebellion.

Impact in the US:
Suspension of this privilege was not done in the US until the Civil War. It has been used sporadically since then but only in US Territories.

Impact on the European Union:
The European Union has proposed establishing a European Criminal Code, which some nations view as a threat to trial by jury, habeas corpus privileges and protection against double jeopardy. In fact, currently, a European Arrest Warrant has been deemed unconstitutional in three member Nations.

Section 2

FEN Constitution Clause:
No legislative act that singles out an individual or group for punishment without a trial, known otherwise as a bill of attainder, shall be passed.

Related US Constitution Clause:
No Bill of Attainder or ex post facto Law shall be passed.

Reason for Clause:
Bills of Attainder were used in England until 1800 and resulted in Parliament ordering the execution of many persons. The New York legislature used a Bill of Attainder during the American Revolution to seize the property of a loyalist. The clause was specifically put in to ensure a complete separation between Congress and the Judiciary.

Impact in the US:
The Supreme Court has invalidated five laws under this clause, the latest being part of the 1947 Taft-Hartley Act making it a crime for a Communist to serve on an executive board of a labor union.

Impact on the European Union:
Since there is no prohibition against a bill of attainder in the EU treaties, such a bill can be passed by the EU parliament.

Section 3

FEN Constitution Clause:
No retroactive law, known otherwise as an ex post facto law, shall be passed.

Related US Constitution Clause:
No Bill of Attainder or ex post facto Law shall be passed.

Reason for Clause:
Some delegates at the Constitutional Convention objected to the clause because it presumes that lawmakers do not know how to legislate. It was found some State constitutions contained the clause.

Impact in the US:
The Supreme Court has determined that the clause applies only to criminal, not civil cases and has established four categories of unconstitutional ex post facto laws:

1) a law making an action taken before the passing of the law, and which was legal when performed, illegal and punishes such action;
2) a law that makes a crime greater than it was when committed;
3) a law inflicting a punishment greater than the law allowed when the crime was committed; or,
4) a law that alters the legal rules of evidence and testimony in place at the time of the commission of the offense.

Impact on the European Union:
In the EU, there is an explicit ban on ex post facto legislation in Article 7 of the European Convention on Human Rights and Article 15 of the International Covenant on Civil and Political Rights.

Section 4

FEN Constitution Clause:
No tax or duty shall be imposed on items exported from any Federation Nation.

Related US Constitution Clause:
No Tax or Duty shall be laid on Articles exported from any State.

Reason for Clause:
The convention delegates at first gave the federal government the sole revenue from taxing imports and exports. However, southern State delegates objected to taxing exports because most of the exports at the time were Southern agricultural products to Europe. An export tax would raise the price of the commodity and hurt the southern economy. Although France taxed the export of wines and brandies and Virginia taxed tobacco exports without hurting their economies.

But, the clause was included because some feared that a Congressional tax on a State's exports might be used to destroy a State's economy.

Impact on the European Union:
The EU has a Customs Union of all EU member nations plus Andorra, Monaco, San Marino and Turkey. Goods moving within this Union do not incur customs duties. However, an export levy may be charged on

specific agricultural products or non-renewable resources shipped to non-EU nations.

Section 5

FEN Constitution Clause:
No regulatory or revenue law shall give preference to the ports of one Federation Nation over another; nor shall any Federation Nation impose an import duty on items imported from any other Federation Nation.

Related US Constitution Clause:
No Preference shall be given by any Regulation of Commerce or Revenue to the Ports of one State over those of another: nor shall Vessels bound to, or from, one State, be obliged to enter, clear, or pay Duties in another.

Reason for Clause:
Some delegates at the Constitutional Convention feared that Congress would require vessels bound for the ports of one State to be first cleared at the port of another State. They struggled with the language until the above was agreed to.

Impact on the European Union:
The EU has no restriction on regulating imports or exports.

Section 6

FEN Constitution Clause:
No money shall be disbursed from the Treasury, unless appropriated by the Assembly in law. An annual accounting of Federation revenues and disbursements shall be published.

Related US Constitution Clause:
No Money shall be drawn from the Treasury, but in Consequence of Appropriations made by Law; and a regular Statement and Account of the Receipts and Expenditures of all public Money shall be published from time to time.

Reason for Clause:
The US Congress passes appropriation laws allowing public expenditures. At the time of the Convention, it was thought impossible to provide an annual accounting of money spent. They agreed that a report every so often would be sufficient.

Impact on the European Union:
In the EU, the Commission proposes an annual budget, which must be agreed to by the Council of Ministers and Parliament. Thereafter, a financial commitment may be made only if there is a line item in the budget authorizing the activity. Under this clause in the FEN Constitution, the Assembly may authorize an expenditure without constraint unless it imposes one on itself.

Section 7

FEN Constitution Clause:
No title of nobility shall be granted by the Federation; and no Person holding any office under the Federation shall accept any gift, office, or title of any kind from any monarch, or foreign country without the consent of the European Assembly.

Related US Constitution Clause:
No Title of Nobility shall be granted by the United States: And no Person holding any Office of Profit or Trust under them, shall, without the Consent of the Congress, accept of any present, Emolument, Office, or Title, of any kind whatever, from any King, Prince, or foreign State.

Reason for Clause:
The clause was inserted to prevent a system of nobility from being established in the US and to protect the government from foreign influence. Titles of Nobility were providing an undeserved aura blinding the people from observing the true character of a person.

Impact in the US:
Notably, during the first session of the Senate, suggestions for addressing the President ranged from 'His Highness, the President of

the United States and Protector of their Liberties,' to 'His Elective Majesty'.

After it was discovered that President Washington was embarrassed by the debate, it was dropped. The current means of address is Mr. President. Congress authorized US armed forces members in World War II to accept decorations, orders, medals and emblems from allied nations up to one year after the war's conclusion.

Congress has passed further acts under this clause allowing gifts from foreign governments under certain conditions.

Impact on the European Union:
No prohibition exists in the EU treaties against granting noble titles, however, a member nation may decide to ignore titles awarded by the EU or other member nations.

Section 8

FEN Constitution Clause:
The Assembly shall make no laws establishing or supporting a religion or religions, or prohibiting the free exercise thereof, or abridging the freedom of speech, or the press, or the right of the People to assemble peaceably and to petition the government for a redress of grievances.

Related US Constitution Clause:
Congress shall make no law respecting an establishment of religion, or prohibiting the free exercise thereof; or abridging the freedom of speech, or of the press; or the right of the people peaceably to assemble, and to petition the Government for a redress of grievances.

Reason for Clause:
The first Amendment to the US Constitution begins the part of the Constitution known as the Bill of Rights. Thomas Jefferson remarked that this Amendment built 'a wall of separation between Church and State.' Religious wars and persecutions in Europe fostered this clause designed to prevent the government from giving exclusive patronage to a religion or sect.

Impact in the US:
Although the Amendment originally applied only to Acts of Congress and not the States, the later 14th Amendment applied this section to the States. Many judicial opinions resulted from this Amendment.

On Religion:
The courts have interpreted the 'establishment' part of the religion clause: If a law has a secular purpose, its primary effect neither advances nor inhibits the free exercise of religion and it does not foster a government entanglement with religion, the law is permissible. The 'free exercise' phrase allows an absolute freedom to believe but a restriction on freedom to act, but religiously motivated conduct must be permitted unless there is a compelling state interest in denying it.

On Speech: Rights have been expanded by the courts to not only protect political speech but anonymous speech, campaign advertising and pornography. The courts have also raised the burden of proof for libel suits over what British Common Law contains, i.e., in the US, a private individual must prove malice to be awarded punitive damages in a libel suit, while public figures have no protection against libel suits.

Pre-publication censorship is prohibited in almost all cases as all speech is allowed unless it presents a 'clear and present danger,' such as yelling 'Fire!' in a crowded theater. Political campaign donations, as a representation of political speech, have some minor restrictions. Some speech has been particularly restricted. For example, commercial speech does not have the same protections as other speech. Commercial speech is defined as speech proposing a commercial transaction, characterized as an advertisement, referencing a specific product and coming from a purveyor having an economic motivation.

Other speech restricted includes students in educational settings. Obscenity and pornography rights also have been somewhat restricted.

On the Press: Courts have allowed laws prohibiting public broadcasters from presenting indecent material. No special taxes on newspapers or magazines is allowed. However, a journalist that is subpoenaed by a grand jury cannot refuse to appear and can be jailed for non-compliance.

On Assembly: This freedom has evolved from a right to protest into a related freedom of association, resulting in the exclusion of persons from a group to maintain the purpose of the group.

The Supreme Court has adjudicated cases applied to this amendment (not a comprehensive list):

Religion. Tax exemptions for religious institutions; Chaplains in legislative bodies; Government sponsored religious displays; Religion in public schools; Prayer in public schools; Government aid to church related schools; Religious institutions functioning as a government agency; Polygamy; Religion and the right to work; Religious tests for public service or benefits; Free exercise of religion and free speech; Free exercise of religion and public education; Solicitation by religious groups; Free exercise of religion and eminent domain; and, Government intervention in church controversies.

Speech. Sedition and imminent danger; False speech; Fighting words; Hecklers; Time, place, and manner of speech; Symbolic speech; Loyalty oaths and affirmations; School speech; Definition of obscenity; Criminal obscenity; Search, seizure and forfeiture of obscene material; Civil and administrative regulation of obscenity; Internet obscenity; Government funded speech; Speech by public employees; Political activity by public employees; and, Commercial speech.

Press. Prior restraint to publication and censorship; Privacy and the press; Taxation and privileges of the press; Defamation; and, Broadcast Media.

Assembly. Freedom of assembly in public forum; and Freedom of association.

Impact on the European Union:
Several nations of the EU have established religions or accord certain privileges to churches. The EU treaties require the EU to respect those

decisions. However, Article 9 of the European Conventions on Human Rights provides everyone the right to freedom of thought, conscience and religion. However, those rights can be limited in the interests of public safety. Although Article 11 of the EU Charter of Fundamental Rights guarantees freedom of expression and information, freedom of the press differs among the EU countries.

Article 12 of the EU Charter of Fundamental Rights guarantees freedom of assembly and association. Interestingly, the EU requires a petition that has 1 million signatures to be considered as a legislative proposal by the European Commission.

Section 9

FEN Constitution Clause:
The right of the People to be secure in their Persons, houses, papers, and effects against unreasonable searches and seizures shall not be violated. No search or arrest warrant shall be issued but upon probable cause, supported by oath or affirmation, particularly describing the place to be searched and the Persons or things to be seized.

Related US Constitution Clause:
The right of the people to be secure in their persons, houses, papers, and effects, against unreasonable searches and seizures, shall not be violated, and no Warrants shall issue, but upon probable cause, supported by Oath or affirmation, and particularly describing the place to be searched, and the persons or things to be seized.

Reason for Clause:
The amendment was added because British courts in the American colonies issued Writs of Assistance (General Search Warrants) to harass the colonists. That is why the definition of a valid warrant is described in detail in this clause.

Impact in the US:
The courts have ruled evidence obtained without a valid warrant is not admissible in court. Until 1961, this clause was applied only to federal and not State law enforcement actions. Since then, the courts have

applied the clause to the States and developed case law dealing with: consent searches, motor vehicle searches, evidence in plain view, border searches, stop and frisk situations, investigatory stops and detentions, reasonable suspicion, and probable cause for a search. A search has occurred, per the courts, when the government obtains information in a situation where a person expects privacy and that expectation is reasonable. A seizure has occurred if a person has been restrained because of force or a show of authority.

Impact on the European Union:
The European Union has a European Evidence Warrant (EEW) used to obtain objects, documents and data for use in criminal proceedings. Unlike the US where only a judicial authority can issue a warrant, a judge, a court, an investigating magistrate or a public prosecutor can issue the EEW.

Section 10

FEN Constitution Clause:
No Person shall be held to answer for a crime that may result in execution or incarceration without an indictment by a grand jury, except for Persons on active duty in the Armed Forces. Moreover, no Person shall be subject to more than one trial for the same offence, or be compelled in any criminal case to be a witness against himself or herself, or be deprived of life, liberty, or property without due process of law. Private property shall not be taken for public use without just compensation.

Related US Constitution Clause:
No person shall be held to answer for a capital, or otherwise infamous crime, unless on a presentment or indictment of a Grand Jury, except in cases arising in the land or naval forces, or in the Militia, when in actual service in time of War or public danger; nor shall any person be subject for the same offence to be twice put in jeopardy of life or limb; nor shall be compelled in any criminal case to be a witness against himself, nor be deprived of life, liberty, or property, without due process of law; nor shall private property be taken for public use, without just compensation.

Reason for Clause:
The grand jury system was designed to prevent vindictive prosecution by the government, political partisans or private enemies.

Impact in the US:
A grand jury's job is to decide if there is enough evidence to prosecute, otherwise known as an indictment. A petit jury is empaneled to try the indicted defendant. A grand jury has fewer restrictions on its procedures than a petit jury, e.g., the rules of evidence are looser and an individual being questioned does not have the right to have an attorney present. The clause does not protect those serving in the Armed Forces or in the State Militia under federal control.
The Double Jeopardy phrase prohibits four types of prosecutions: 1) prosecution for the same crime after acquittal; 2) prosecution for additional punishment after conviction; 3) prosecution after certain mistrials; and 4) multiple punishments in the same indictment. The Self-Incrimination right applies when an individual testifies in a legal proceeding, federal or state, criminal or civil. Better known as the Miranda warning, US detective TV shows and movies portray it when a person arrested is told that he or she has the right to remain silent, and any statement he or she makes may be used against him or her in a court of law.

The due process phrase provides several rights applicable to all government actions that can result in a person's civil or criminal prosecution: 1) an unbiased tribunal; 2) notice of the proposed action and the grounds for it; 3) the opportunity to present reasons why the proposed action should not be taken; 4) the right to present evidence and call witnesses; 5) the right to know opposing evidence; 6) the right to cross-examine adverse witnesses; 7) a decision based solely on the evidence presented; 8) the opportunity to be represented by counsel; 9) a requirement for a record of the evidence presented; and, 10) a requirement that the tribunal prepare written findings of fact and reasons for its decision.

The takings clause provides the federal government and each State the power of eminent domain to take private property for public use.

However, the government must give the owner fair market value for the property.

Impact on the European Union:
In the EU, the rights of the accused in criminal prosecutions vary. 'The Roadmap for Strengthening Procedural Rights of Suspected or Accused Persons in Criminal Proceedings', a goal to unify criminal procedure in the EU does not address the need for separate indictments, does not prohibit double jeopardy, or self-incrimination.

Section 11

FEN Constitution Clause:
In all criminal prosecutions, the accused shall have a speedy and public trial by an impartial jury composed of Citizens of the Nation and district where the crime was committed, the district having been previously established by law. The accused shall be informed of the nature and cause of the accusation, can confront the prosecution witnesses, have a compulsory process for obtaining witnesses in his or her favor, and have the assistance of legal counsel for his or her defense. All criminal convictions shall require a unanimous jury verdict.

Related US Constitution Clause:
In all criminal prosecutions, the accused shall enjoy the right to a speedy and public trial, by an impartial jury of the State and district wherein the crime shall have been committed, which district shall have been previously ascertained by law, and to be informed of the nature and cause of the accusation; to be confronted with the witnesses against him; to have compulsory process for obtaining witnesses in his favor, and to have the Assistance of Counsel for his defence.

Reason for Clause:
This clause provides the protections all criminal defendants have in the US.

Impact in the US:
Speedy Trial – The US courts have developed the criteria used to determine when a defendant's right to a speedy trial has been violated:

Length of delay; Reason for Delay; Agreement by Defendant; and, Damage to the Defendant. For violating this right, charges must be dismissed or a conviction must be overturned.

Public Trial – Limits on public access to a trial have been approved by the courts if publicity would weaken the defendant's right to a fair trial.

Impartial Jury – For offenses that may be punishable by six months or less imprisonment, a jury trial is not required. Minors are tried in juvenile court without a jury. Jurys can vary from six to 12 persons. The jury pool must represent the community where the crime was committed. Jurors may be questioned to determine any bias.

Notice of Accusation – The indictment must include sufficient detail so the defendant can claim double jeopardy if a subsequent prosecution on the same charge is made.

Confronting Witnesses – All testimony must be capable of direct challenge. No hearsay evidence is permitted, i.e., a witness cannot refer to the statements of another person who cannot be directly challenged in court. All physical evidence must be presented to the defense for examination before presenting it to the jury.

Compulsory Process – A witness can be compelled to testify in court.

Assistance of Counsel – The court must provide counsel to those unable to mount a defense because of illiteracy, ignorance or penury. The rule applies to all those arrested and interrogated by law enforcement. A defendant may choose to represent him or herself unless the court rules him or her incompetent.

The US Supreme Court has issued opinions on (not comprehensive): speedy trial definition; public trial definition; availability of the jury; impartiality; size and unanimity of the jury; out of court statements; face to face confrontation; restrictions on cross examination; right to present relevant evidence; compulsory process; choice of counsel; appointment of counsel; ineffective counsel; and self-representation.

Impact on the European Union:
The EU has no role in criminal proceedings in Member Nations. Each nation has its own rules. However, Article 6 of the European Convention on Human Rights stipulates that the right to a fair trial implies the accused and citizens must understand the verdict and the reasons for it. Since a jury does not provide reasons for its decisions, the Article does not guarantee trial by jury.

In fact, the Corpus Juris, a procedure developed to deal with fraud involving EU funds, could be used to transfer control over criminal procedure from member nations to the EU. The Corpus Juris does not allow for trial by jury.

Section 12

FEN Constitution Clause:
In civil lawsuits where the value in controversy exceeds an amount determined by the Assembly, the right of trial by jury shall be preserved, and no fact tried by a jury shall be otherwise re-examined in any court of the Federation unless a retrial is conducted.

Related US Constitution Clause:
In Suits at common law, where the value in controversy shall exceed twenty dollars, the right of trial by jury shall be preserved, and no fact tried by a jury, shall be otherwise re-examined in any Court of the United States, than according to the rules of the common law.

Reason for Clause:
The 'twenty dollar' amount for a jury trial has never been adjusted, but in any case, $75,000 is the minimum that must be at stake for a federal jury trial to be conducted.

Impact in the US:
The Supreme Court has ruled the minimum jury size is six and the verdict in a jury trial must be unanimous.

Impact on the European Union:
Article 6 of the European Convention of Human Rights provides the same rights to a civil defendant as a criminal defendant, but does not include the right to a jury trial. However, the EU does not have judicial authority over civil actions within EU nations unless the action involves an EU decision or action.

Section 13

FEN Constitution Clause:
Excessive bail shall not be required, nor excessive fines imposed, nor cruel and unusual punishments inflicted, all as defined by the Assembly in law. The death penalty shall not be imposed by the Federation, or by any Member Nation or other jurisdiction within the Federation.

Related US Constitution Clause:
Excessive bail shall not be required, nor excessive fines imposed, nor cruel and unusual punishments inflicted.

Impact in the US:
US courts have ruled that a bail amount is excessive if the amount is 'higher than is reasonably calculated' to ensure the defendant's appearance for trial. However, bail may be denied if the charges are serious and the accused Is a flight risk. Any fine imposed must be proportional to the gravity of the offense. A cruel and unusual punishment has been defined as: 1) degrading human dignity or is considered torture; 2) arbitrary; 3) clearly and totally rejected throughout society; and, 4) patently unnecessary.

In specific cases, the courts have determined that drawing and quartering, public dissection, burning at the stake, disembowelment, execution of the mentally handicapped and persons under 18, removing citizenship of a natural born citizen, shackling during incarceration, permanently denying civil rights, life without parole for a minor, and the death penalty for a crime in which death does not occur are cruel and unusual punishments.

US States and the federal government have authority to apply capital punishment but the types vary by State from lethal injection, electrocution, gas chamber, hanging and firing squad.

Impact on the European Union:
In the EU, criminal procedure is governed by the member nations. However, member nations must abolish the death penalty as a condition of membership in the EU.

Section 14

FEN Constitution Clause:
The enumeration in this Constitution of certain rights shall not be interpreted as denying or disparaging others retained by the People of the Federation.

Related US Constitution Clause:
The enumeration in the Constitution, of certain rights, shall not be construed to deny or disparage others retained by the people.

Reason for Clause:
During the US Constitution ratification process, several States wanted a specific Bill of Rights added to the Constitution. Those against such a bill maintained such a list could, in effect, give the Congress power to act in those areas not mentioned in the list. This clause was added to ensure that rights not mentioned in the Constitution could not be denied simply because they were not mentioned.

Section 15

FEN Constitution Clause:
The powers not given to the Federation by this Constitution, nor prohibited by it to Federation Nations, are reserved for the Nations or for the People of the Federation.

Related US Constitution Clause:
The powers not delegated to the United States by the Constitution, nor prohibited by it to the States, are reserved to the States respectively, or to the people.

Reason for Clause:
James Madison felt the national government's powers were few and defined and would be focused on external items such as war, foreign relations, international treaties and commerce. In his mind, the States would have the most extensive powers and the most contact with US citizens during their lives. To ensure this separation of powers, this clause was added. In effect, a power not given to the Federal Government and not withheld to the States belongs to the States or the people.

Impact on the European Union:
In the EU, each member nation is sovereign and is not beholden to any other. Each considers its laws as above those of any nation including those passed by the EU. In fact, EU laws are not effective in themselves, but only become effective when passed by the legislature in each member nation and only for that member nation. Under the FEN, laws would have immediate effect in all member nations.

Article 10 – Limits on Federation Nations
Section 1

FEN Constitution Clause:
No Nation shall enter into any treaty, alliance or confederation, coin money or issue currency, make anything but Federation currency or coin legal tender, pass any retroactive law, or a law singling out an individual or group for punishment without a trial, or a law that impairs the obligations of a legal contract.

Related US Constitution Clause:
No State shall enter into any Treaty, Alliance, or Confederation; grant Letters of Marque and Reprisal; coin Money; emit Bills of Credit; make any Thing but gold and silver Coin a Tender in Payment of Debts; pass

any Bill of Attainder, ex post facto Law, or Law impairing the Obligation of Contracts, or grant any Title of Nobility.

Reason for Clause:
This section prevents the States from exercising any authority reserved exclusively for the federal government, including conducting international affairs, and issuing coin or currency. It also includes the same prohibitions against ex post facto laws, bills of attainder and interference with contracts as the federal government has.

Impact in the US:
The phrase on obligations of contracts generated a controversial Supreme Court case, Fletcher vs Peck. In Georgia, corrupt members of the Georgia legislature were bribed to authorize the sale of public lands to speculators at low prices. The next elected legislature rescinded the land sales, but the Supreme Court ruled the sale was the result of a valid contract and could not be rescinded even though it was corrupt.

Impact on the European Union:
Although the Euro is the official currency of the European Union, not every member nation has it as its currency. Under the FEN, all member nations would have to support a common currency. Unlike the US where titles of nobility are prohibited, FEN member nations (but not the FEN) could still issue titles of nobility.

Section 2

FEN Constitution Clause:
No Nation shall impose a duty on imports, exports, or weight beyond those charges necessary to fund the basic cost of its inspection laws without the approval of the Assembly. All such charges shall be subject to the control of the Assembly.

Related US Constitution Clause:
No State shall, without the Consent of the Congress, lay any Imposts or Duties on Imports or Exports, except what may be absolutely necessary for executing it's inspection Laws: and the net Produce of all Duties and Imposts, laid by any State on Imports or Exports, shall be for the Use of

the Treasury of the United States; and all such Laws shall be subject to the Revision and Controul of the Congress.

Reason for Clause:
In effect, a State cannot place a duty on an import or export greater than an amount needed to fund necessary inspection costs. The clause was added to prevent a State from taxing products of another State that passed through its territory or taxing the exported products of its own manufacturers.

Impact in the US:
On this subject, the Supreme Court has stated the clause only applies to imports in containers or wrapping as delivered to the importer. Once the imported products become mixed with other property, the State could regulate or tax them. The Supreme Court also declared a Maryland law, passed without the consent of Congress, unconstitutional because it required an importer to obtain a State license.

Impact on the European Union:
This clause would have a great impact on the EU since it would require all import duties into member nations be sent to the Federation Treasury.

Section 3

FEN Constitution Clause:
No Nation shall, without the consent of the Assembly, keep an Armed Force independent of the Federation Armed Forces nor enter into any agreement with another Federation Nation or foreign power, nor engage in war unless invaded or in imminent danger of invasion.

Related US Constitution Clause:
No State shall, without the Consent of Congress, lay any Duty of Tonnage, keep Troops, or Ships of War in time of Peace, enter into any Agreement or Compact with another State, or with a foreign Power, or engage in War, unless actually invaded, or in such imminent Danger as will not admit of delay.

Reason for Clause:
The Constitutional Convention inserted this clause to keep the States out of the international arena and prevent them from building up a naval or land force except for their militia. To prevent a cabal of States acting against the federal government, compacts between States are disallowed unless approved by the Congress.

Impact in the US:
The courts have determined the clause applies only when an interstate compact would increase the political power of the States versus the federal government.

Impact on the European Union:
Although the EU does not have an independent armed force, this clause would provide control of the Armed Forces of member nations as the FEN Assembly directs. It would also abolish all the foreign ministries of the member nations and give complete international affairs control to the Federation.

Section 4

FEN Constitution Clause:
The right of Federation Citizens who are 18 years of age or older, to vote, shall not be denied or reduced by the Federation or a Member Nation because of race, color, gender, religious belief, or failure to pay any tax.

Related US Constitution Clauses:
The right of citizens of the United States to vote shall not be denied or abridged by the United States or by any State on account of race, color, or previous condition of servitude.

The right of citizens of the United States to vote shall not be denied or abridged by the United States or by any State on account of sex.

The right of citizens of the United States to vote in any primary or other election for President or Vice President, for electors for President or Vice President, or for Senator or Representative in Congress, shall not be denied or abridged by the United States or any state by reason of failure to pay any poll tax or other tax.

The right of citizens of the United States, who are 18 years of age or older, to vote, shall not be denied or abridged by the United States or any state on account of age.

Impact in the US:
The US Constitution gives the States the right to determine voting qualifications. Universal white male suffrage was the mode up to the Civil War. Neither women, free blacks nor slaves could vote in most States.

The 15th Amendment to the Constitution provided voting rights to free black men and former male slaves, but the Southern States got around the criteria by requiring payment of a tax to vote or requiring literacy tests.

The Women's Suffrage Movement secured the passage of the 19th Amendment providing women the right to vote, while the 24th Amendment abolished poll taxes and the Voting Rights Act of 1965 banned literacy tests. The 26th Amendment lowered the voting age to 18.

Impact on the European Union:
In the EU, each nation determines its voting qualifications but the FEN will endow those rights to all citizens over the age of 18.

Section 5

FEN Constitution Clause:
No money raised by taxation in any Nation for the support of public schools, or derived from any public fund for that purpose, nor any public lands devoted thereto, shall ever be under the control of any religious sect; nor shall any money so raised or lands so devoted be provided to religious sects or denominations.

Related US Constitution Clause:
No Reference.

Impact in the US:
President Grant proposed to a group of veterans in 1875 a Constitutional amendment prohibiting public funds to be used to support private religious schools. He maintained that religion and government should be forever separate and religion should be left to families, churches and private schools. It failed to pass Congress, but thirty-nine states have versions of this amendment in their constitutions.

The issue is whether a person should be forced to support with his or her tax dollars the religious beliefs of a sect they do not believe in.

Impact on the European Union:
Under the FEN, this paragraph would prohibit Great Britain, Denmark and Greece from supporting not only their State church schools but also their State religion.

Chapter II – The Executive
Article 1 – The President and Vice President
Section 1

FEN Constitution Clause:
The executive power shall be vested in a President of the Federation of European Nations. The President shall hold the office for a term of six years, and, together with the Vice President, chosen for the same term, shall be elected as follows:

Related US Constitution Clause:
The executive Power shall be vested in a President of the United States of America. He shall hold his Office during the Term of four Years, and, together with the Vice President, chosen for the same Term, be elected, as follows

Reason for Clause:
The Constitutional Convention's original thought was that the National Legislature, like the British parliamentary system, would select the National Executive. Experience with the English King soured some delegates on a single executive as tending to monarchical powers. They wanted the National Executive to be a group of individuals like the Executive group running the national government under the Articles of Confederation. Others wanted a dual executive to avoid appearance of a monarchy, but objectors cited the example of the dual executives in the Roman and Greek Republics that led to their demise. Some wanted a three-person executive council, one for each area of the country. Others claimed three chiefs in a war situation would prove disastrous. A legislature must have differing opinions and questioning of plans and motives to ensure a good law, but an executive must be able to act as needed within authority without having to negotiate with someone of equal authority. Eventually, a single person as executive was agreed upon, because most delegates knew the first President would be George Washington, a man they trusted. Also, since each State had a single executive as Governor, they agreed that such an arrangement would be natural at the national level.

The discussion on the President's term of office started with seven years. A term of three years was examined with a prohibition of reelection championed by those who were against a strong executive. Considered also were eleven, 15, and 20 year terms (the average life of princes.) They finally agreed not to limit the number of terms a person could serve along with a four-year term.

Since presiding officers normally do not have voting powers in a legislature, the position of Vice President to preside over the Senate was established to ensure no State would be deprived of its vote when one of its members was selected to preside.

Impact on the European Union:
The European Commission is considered the executive arm of the European Union. The Commission's President serves a five-year term.

Clause a

FEN Constitution Clause:
Each Nation shall select, based on rules established by its Legislature, a number of Electors, equal to the number of Senators and Delegates they are entitled to in the European Assembly. The Assembly may determine the schedule for choosing the Electors, and their voting day that shall be uniform throughout the Federation. No Senator, Delegate, or Person holding office of any kind under the Federation, or Person not born in the respective Nation shall be appointed an Elector.

Related US Constitution Clause:
Each State shall appoint, in such Manner as the Legislature thereof may direct, a Number of Electors, equal to the whole Number of Senators and Representatives to which the State may be entitled in the Congress: but no Senator or Representative, or Person holding an Office of Trust or Profit under the United States, shall be appointed an Elector.

Reason for Clause:
The President and Vice President of the US are chosen not by a popular vote of the people but by State electors, selected per rules established by each State legislature. The Constitutional Convention came to this plan after several other proposals to elect the President came forth including election by Congress, State governors, and State legislatures. To avoid any political chicanery in electing a President, an organization established just to elect the chief executive and then disbanded was thought most proper: The Electoral College.

The legislatures of the States were thought to be closest to the will of the people and were entrusted with making the rules for this organization of electors, ensuring the people would have the greatest say on a position where trust was most needed.

Impact in the US:
Early on, most legislatures selected the electors directly, but since the early 19th century, the electors have been selected via popular vote in which an elector is the 'stand in' for the true candidate. In any case, an elector, even if pledged to vote for a certain candidate, can vote for

anyone on voting day. To prevent any undue influence on an elector, he or she cannot hold any national office.

Impact on the European Union:
In the EU, the European Council selects the President of the European Commission.

Clause b

FEN Constitution Clause:
The Electors shall meet in their respective Nations and vote by ballot for President and Vice-President, one of whom, at least, shall not have been born in the same Nation as themselves. They shall name in one ballot the Person voted for as President, and in another ballot the Person voted for as Vice President, and they shall make separate lists of all Persons voted for as President, and of all Persons voted for as Vice President, and of the number of votes for each. The Electors shall sign and certify the lists and transmit them sealed to the seat of the government of the Federation of European Nations, directed to the Speaker of the Chamber of Delegates.

Related US Constitution Clause:
The Electors shall meet in their respective states, and vote by ballot for President and Vice-President, one of whom, at least, shall not be an inhabitant of the same state with themselves; they shall name in their ballots the person voted for as President, and in distinct ballots the person voted for as Vice-President, and they shall make distinct lists of all persons voted for as President, and of all persons voted for as Vice-President, and of the number of votes for each, which lists they shall sign and certify, and transmit sealed to the seat of the government of the United States, directed to the President of the Senate...

Reason for Clause:
The language cited above is from the 12th Amendment to the US Constitution. The reason the electors meet in their own States was to prevent exposure to political pressures if meeting in the national capital. The original language had each elector submit two ballots for President. It was thought that if an elector chose only one candidate,

each State would select a native son for President. Asking the elector to select someone with a second ballot encouraged him to perhaps select a national figure from another state. The person who received the second most votes was to be the Vice President.

Impact in the US:
The original system worked well for the first US Presidential election as George Washington received an electoral vote from each elector, while 11 others received at least one vote. The same thing happened in the second election as Washington again won but only four other candidates received votes. However, political parties had begun to form around certain candidates. In the third election, John Adams of Massachusetts received two votes over the required majority to claim the office over Thomas Jefferson. Eleven other candidates also received votes. But Jefferson did secure the Vice Presidency under the rules and with it the duty of head of the Senate.

Since Adams and Jefferson did not get along at the time, a power struggle between them hurt development of the national government. But the fourth election (in 1800) showed the real flaw in the procedure eventually requiring a Constitutional Amendment to correct (See next clause).

Impact on the European Union:
Currently, the heads of state or governments of EU nations propose the President of the European Commission to the EU Parliament for an up or down vote. The European people have no input on their Chief Executive. Under the FEN Constitution, the legislatures of each Nation will develop procedures to choose the EU President electors, making the winner more representative of the people.

Clause c

FEN Constitution Clause:
The Speaker of the Chamber, in the presence of the Senators and Delegates, shall open all the certified lists and the votes shall then be counted. The Person having the greatest number of votes for President shall be the President, if the number of votes is a majority of the whole

number of Electors appointed. If no Person has such a majority, then from the Persons having the three highest numbers of votes on the list of those voted for as President, the Chamber shall choose immediately, by ballot, the President. However, in choosing the President, the votes shall be taken by Nations, the representation from each Nation having one vote. A quorum for this purpose shall consist of at least one Delegate from two-thirds of the Nations, and a majority of all the Nations shall be necessary to a choice.

Related US Constitution Clause:
The President of the Senate shall, in the presence of the Senate and House of Representatives, open all the certificates and the votes shall then be counted;—The person having the greatest number of votes for President, shall be the President, if such number be a majority of the whole number of Electors appointed; and if no person have such majority, then from the persons having the highest numbers not exceeding three on the list of those voted for as President, the House of Representatives shall choose immediately, by ballot, the President. But in choosing the President, the votes shall be taken by states, the representation from each state having one vote; a quorum for this purpose shall consist of a member or members from two-thirds of the states, and a majority of all the states shall be necessary to a choice.

Reason for Clause:
The framers of the Constitution assumed that each State's electors would vote for a resident of their state as President in effect leaving 13 candidates all lacking a majority, requiring an alternate method of selection. The alternate method selected above was objected to by the larger States who said giving each State one vote would give the same voting weight to the small States as the larger ones. However, the counter argument maintained that advantage would be offset by the larger State's candidates who would have more electoral votes and be among the top three to be considered by the House.

Impact in the US: Although the rise of political parties and national candidates have removed the need for this procedure, in the early years of the US, the candidates in two elections failed to garner the necessary majority of electors and required this procedure. The language of this clause above was amended by the situation that occurred in the Election of 1800.

The original clause specified each elector would submit two ballots, ostensibly one for President and one for Vice President, but there would be no distinction between the two ballots. They would all be counted, the most votes would be President, then next most Vice President, provided the winning candidate had the majority of electors.

In 1800, the Democratic-Republicans were an organized party, headed by Thomas Jefferson. The election plan was for the Democratic-Republican electors to place Jefferson's name on half of their ballots and Aaron Burr's name (a prominent New York Democratic-Republican) on the remaining ballots except one, to allow Jefferson to be President and Burr Vice President, having one less vote than Jefferson.

What happened is that electors from 9 states placed Jefferson's and Burr's name on both ballots. Consequently, both Jefferson and Burr wound up with an equal number of votes, throwing the election into the House of Representatives. It took almost two months and 36 votes for the House to break the tie and choose Jefferson as President, since Burr declined to withdraw his name. To avoid the same situation, the 12th Amendment was passed to give the elector a separate choice for President and a separate choice for Vice President.

The change denigrated the office of Vice President. Under the original procedure, the person getting the second most votes was considered to be worthy of being President. These days, the Vice Presidential candidate is selected by the Presidential candidate to balance the ticket for geographic religious or political reasons and has usually been seen as lower in ability than the President.

In the Election of 1824, regional interests split the popular vote among four candidates. The House chose to elect the President and chose the person Adams, who had the second most electoral votes, over Jackson who had the most. That was the last election decided in the House.

Impact on the European Union:
The European Parliament of the EU approves the President of the European Commission as proposed by the European Council.

Clause d

FEN Constitution Clause:
The Person having the greatest number of votes for Vice President shall be the Vice President, if the number of votes is a majority of the whole number of Electors appointed. If no Person has a majority, then from the Persons having the two highest numbers of votes on the list of those voted for as Vice President, the Senate shall choose the Vice President. A quorum for the purpose shall consist of two-thirds of the whole number of Senators, and a majority of the whole number shall be necessary to a choice.

Related US Constitution Clause:
The person having the greatest number of votes as Vice-President, shall be the Vice-President, if such number be a majority of the whole number of Electors appointed, and if no person have a majority, then from the two highest numbers on the list, the Senate shall choose the Vice-President; a quorum for the purpose shall consist of two-thirds of the whole number of Senators, and a majority of the whole number shall be necessary to a choice.

Reason for Clause:
This election method is like that of the President.

Impact on the European Union:
Two Vice Presidents serve in the EU. The First Vice President is also the High Representative of the Union for Foreign Affairs and Security Policy. A majority of the European Council appoints the High Representative but ascension to the post of Vice President requires approval by Parliament. The Commission President appoints the Second Vice President.

Clause e

FEN Constitution Clause:
The Assembly may, by law, provide for the case of the death of any of the Persons from whom the Assembly may choose as President whenever the right of choice shall have devolved upon them, and for the case of the death of any of the Persons from whom the Senate may choose as Vice President whenever the right of choice shall have devolved upon them.

Related US Constitution Clause:
The Congress may by law provide for the case of the death of any of the persons from whom the House of Representatives may choose a President whenever the right of choice shall have devolved upon them, and for the case of the death of any of the persons from whom the Senate may choose a Vice President whenever the right of choice shall have devolved upon them.

Reason for Clause:
The clause provides a solution to a potential situation.

Impact in the US:
Congress has never enacted a law to implement this authority perhaps thinking the situation may never arise.

Impact on the European Union:
The clause has no effect in the EU since the choice of a President would never meet the situation described.

Clause f

FEN Constitution Clause:
If a President has not been chosen before the time fixed for the beginning of the President's term, the Vice President-elect shall act as President until a President has been chosen. The Assembly may, by law, provide for the case wherein neither a President-elect or a Vice President-elect has been chosen, declaring who shall then act as

President, or the manner in which one is to act shall be selected, and such Person shall act accordingly until a President or Vice President has been chosen.

Related US Constitution Clause:
If, at the time fixed for the beginning of the term of the President, the President elect shall have died, the Vice President elect shall become President. If a President shall not have been chosen before the time fixed for the beginning of his term, or if the President elect shall have failed to qualify, then the Vice President elect shall act as President until a President shall have qualified; and the Congress may by law provide for the case wherein neither a President elect nor a Vice President elect shall have qualified, declaring who shall then act as President, or the manner in which one who is to act shall be selected, and such person shall act accordingly until a President or Vice President shall have qualified.

Reason for Clause:
This clause was part of the Twentieth Amendment and gives the Congress the right to determine by law who would act as President if one has not been selected in time.

Impact in the US: Congress passed the Third Presidential Succession Act in 1947 to implement this clause.

Impact on the European Union:
The clause has no effect in the EU since the choice of a President would never meet the situation described.

Section 2

FEN Constitution Clause:
No Person constitutionally ineligible to the office of President shall be eligible to that of Vice President and no Person shall be elected to the office of the President more than twice.

Related US Constitution Clause:
But no person constitutionally ineligible to the office of President shall be eligible to that of Vice-President of the United States.

No person shall be elected to the office of the President more than twice, and no person who has held the office of President, or acted as President, for more than two years of a term to which some other person was elected President shall be elected to the office of the President more than once. But this article shall not apply to any person holding the office of President when this article was proposed by the Congress, and shall not prevent any person who may be holding the office of President, or acting as President, during the term within which this article becomes operative from holding the office of President or acting as President during the remainder of such term.

Reason for Clause:
Since the Vice President can succeed a President who dies in office, resigns or is removed, he or she obviously must possess the same qualifications as the President.

Impact in the US:
The term limit for the President was ostensibly designed to prevent a monarchy or dictatorship, but it was done by a Republican Congress to prevent a Roosevelt four term recurrence. The US followed the standard set by George Washington of two terms but Franklin Roosevelt broke the pattern.

Impact on the European Union:
No restriction exists on the number of terms the President of the European Commission can serve.

Section 3

FEN Constitution Clause:
The President must have been born in a Federation Nation, must be 35 years old at the time of election, and must have been a resident of a Federation Nation for at least 15 years.

Related US Constitution Clause:
No Person except a natural born Citizen, or a Citizen of the United States, at the time of the Adoption of this Constitution, shall be eligible to the Office of President; neither shall any Person be eligible to that

Office who shall not have attained to the Age of thirty five Years, and been fourteen Years a Resident within the United States.

Reason for Clause:
The clause eliminates naturalized citizens from being President of the FEN and requires the President to have lived in a Federation Nation for at least 15 years.

Impact in the US: The phrase natural born citizen has never been defined by the courts. Several presidential candidates were born in US Territories, or in a foreign country casting doubt on their qualifications for the office, but none were elected to the office.

Impact on the European Union:
No specific qualifications to be President of the European Commission of the EU are contained in the treaties but certain criteria must be considered.

Section 4

FEN Constitution Clause:
The President shall receive a salary set by the Assembly that cannot be increased or decreased during the President's term of office. The President shall not receive within that term of office any other compensation or gift from the Federation or any of its Nations.

Related US Constitution Clause:
The President shall, at stated Times, receive for his Services, a Compensation, which shall neither be encreased nor diminished during the Period for which he shall have been elected, and he shall not receive within that Period any other Emolument from the United States, or any of them.

Reason for Clause:
Benjamin Franklin proposed at the Constitutional Convention no salary for the President but only reimbursement of his expenses. That was too open ended for the Convention and would have tended to attract only the wealthy to the office. Requiring the President's salary not be

changed during his term was to prevent the legislature from punishing or bribing the President. Preventing a State from paying the President also eliminated the possibility of one State buying influence.

Impact in the US:
The US President's salary is currently $400,000 a year.

Impact on the European Union:
The Salary of the EU Commission President is based on the top civil service grade.

Section 5

FEN Constitution Clause:
Before assuming the duties of the office, the President shall take the following oath or affirmation in the presence of the Assembly: "I do solemnly swear (or affirm) that I will faithfully execute the Office of President of the Federation of European Nations, and will, to the best of my ability, preserve, protect, and defend the Constitution of the Federation of European Nations."

Related US Constitution Clause:
Before he enter on the Execution of his Office, he shall take the following Oath or Affirmation:— "I do solemnly swear (or affirm) that I will faithfully execute the Office of President of the United States, and will to the best of my Ability, preserve, protect and defend the Constitution of the United States."

Reason for Clause:
The first draft of the Constitution presented to the Convention left the wording of the oath up to the first Congress. The Convention, however, determined the wording of the oath and placed it in the Constitution.

Impact in the US:
The President-Elect adds his name after the word 'I'. Notably, the oath requires the President to defend the Constitution, not the nation. Some have interpreted it to mean the President may decline to enforce laws he or she believes are unconstitutional. The oath is usually administered

by the Chief Justice of the US Supreme Court on the steps of the Capitol, symbolically conferring legitimacy on the new President by including the other branches of the government at his or her inauguration.

Impact on the European Union:
EU Commissioners upon taking office take an oath at the European Court of Justice as follows:

"Having been appointed as a Member of the European Commission by the European Council, following the vote of consent by the European Parliament,

I solemnly undertake: to respect the Treaties and the Charter of Fundamental Rights of the European Union in the fulfilment of all my duties; to be completely independent in carrying out my responsibilities, in the general interest of the Union; in the performance of my tasks, neither to seek nor to take instructions from any Government or from any other institution, body, office or entity; to refrain from any action incompatible with my duties or the performance of my tasks.

I formally note the undertaking of each Member State to respect this principle and not to seek to influence Members of the Commission in the performance of their tasks.

I further undertake to respect, both during and after my term of office, the obligation arising therefrom, and in particular the duty to behave with integrity and discretion as regards the acceptance, after I have ceased to hold office, of certain appointments or benefits."

Section 6

FEN Constitution Clause:
The terms of the President and Vice President shall end at noon on the 8th day of May of the year the term is to end, when the terms of their successors will begin. If, at the time fixed for the beginning of the term of the President, the President-elect shall have died, the Vice President-elect shall become President.

Related US Constitution Clause:
The terms of the President and Vice President shall end at noon on the 20th day of January, and the terms of Senators and Representatives at noon on the 3d day of January, of the years in which such terms would have ended if this article had not been ratified; and the terms of their successors shall then begin.

If, at the time fixed for the beginning of the term of the President, the President elect shall have died, the Vice President elect shall become President.

Reason for Clause:
The US Constitution originally required Congress to meet annually on the first Monday in December but also allowed Congress to set another date by law. After the Constitution had been ratified in June 1788, the disbanding Confederation Congress set the formation date for the new government as March 4, 1789, also determining the starting date of the Presidential and Congressional terms. The newly elected First Congress of the United States achieved a quorum and met in its first session on April 6 wherein the electoral votes were counted that elected George Washington the first President.

Impact in the US:
Later, the Congress passed a law designating Presidential electors to be chosen in November every four years. Since the Presidential term ended in March, any new President elected in November had to wait until the following March to be inaugurated as did the new Congress.

Consequently, the Constitutional requirement to meet on the first Monday in December required the old Congress to meet then and the newly elected Congress to meet the following year in December. In the 19th century, such an arrangement was necessary as travel over primitive roads required time to reach Washington DC.

However, crises threatening the nation could not be dealt with in a timely manner. Both Abraham Lincoln and Franklin Roosevelt had to wait four months to assume office to deal with the Southern Secession crisis and the Great Depression respectively.

Impact on the European Union:
In the European Union, the President of the European Commission is elected for a renewable five-year term that begins six months after European Parliament elections in the years ending in 4 and 9.

Section 7

FEN Constitution Clause:
If the President is removed from office, dies, resigns, or is unable to discharge the powers and duties of the office, the Vice President shall become President. The Assembly, by law, may provide a further line of succession in case of removal, death, resignation, or inability to discharge the powers and duties of the office, of both the President and Vice President. In no case, however, will a by-election be held to fill a vacancy in the Presidential office.

Related US Constitution Clause:
In Case of the Removal of the President from Office, or of his Death, Resignation, or Inability to discharge the Powers and Duties of the said Office, the Same shall devolve on the Vice President, and the Congress may by Law provide for the Case of Removal, Death, Resignation or Inability, both of the President and Vice President, declaring what Officer shall then act as President, and such Officer shall act accordingly, until the Disability be removed, or a President shall be elected.

Reason for Clause:
Several solutions were proposed during the Constitutional Convention on the problem of a Presidential vacancy. After considering proposals to have the President of the Senate or the Chief Justice of the Supreme Court take over, the Office of the Vice President was established as a solution. However, the above clause of the US Constitution on this subject did not stipulate who would determine whether the President was unable to discharge his authority.

The clause also did not address a Vice Presidential vacancy, nor the situation when a President or Vice President had not been elected.

Impact in the US:
The position of Vice President has been vacant 16 times in US history. The 25th Amendment resolved all the above issues. Congress has also passed laws designating the order of succession if both offices become vacant.

Impact on the European Union:
The EU has a policy designating one of the Vice Presidents to replace a Commission President upon removal, death, resignation or inability of the incumbent from performing his or her duties.

Section 8

FEN Constitution Clause:
Whenever there is a vacancy in the office of the Vice President, the President shall nominate a Vice President who shall take office upon confirmation by a majority vote of both Houses of the Assembly.

Related US Constitution Clause:
Whenever there is a vacancy in the office of the Vice President, the President shall nominate a Vice President who shall take office upon confirmation by a majority vote of both Houses of Congress.

Reason for Clause:
The US Vice Presidency has been vacant 16 times because of the death or resignation of the President or Vice President.

Impact in the US:
The procedure has been used twice since then.

Impact on the European Union:
The EU Commission President, with the approval of the Commission, can fill a vacancy in the office of Vice President of the Commission.

Section 9

FEN Constitution Clause:
Whenever the President transmits to the Vice President and the Speaker of the Chamber of Delegates a written declaration that he or she is unable to discharge the powers and duties of the office, and until he or she transmits to them a written declaration to the contrary, such powers and duties shall be discharged by the Vice President as Acting President.

Related US Constitution Clause:
Whenever the President transmits to the President pro tempore of the Senate and the Speaker of the House of Representatives his written declaration that he is unable to discharge the powers and duties of his office, and until he transmits to them a written declaration to the contrary, such powers and duties shall be discharged by the Vice President as Acting President.

Reason for Clause: This clause would allow an ill President to transfer his authority to ensure continuity of operations but it does not address the situation where an incapacitated President cannot transmit a written declaration.

Impact in the US:
The three times this clause was invoked was about the President undergoing anesthesia during surgery.

Impact on the European Union:
The EU treaty stipulates one of the Vice-Presidents will replace a Commission President unable to discharge his duties.

Section 10

FEN Constitution Clause:
Whenever the Vice President and a majority of either the principal officers of the executive departments, or of such other body as the Assembly may by law provide, transmit to the Senate and the Speaker

of the Chamber of Delegates their written declaration that the President is unable to discharge the powers and duties of his or her office, the Assembly shall decide the issue, meeting within forty-eight hours for that purpose. If the Assembly, within twenty-one days after receipt of the latter written declaration, determines by two-thirds vote of both Houses that the President is unable to discharge the powers and duties of his or her office, the Vice President shall discharge the same as Acting President; otherwise, the President shall continue to execute the powers and duties of his or her office. If, after such determination, the President transmits to the President pro tempore of the Senate and the Speaker of the Chamber of Delegates his or her written declaration that no inability exists, the Assembly shall decide the issue, meeting within forty-eight hours. If the Assembly, within twenty-one days after receipt of the President's written declaration, determines by two-thirds vote of both Houses that the President is able to discharge the powers and duties of his or her office, the President shall resume the powers and duties of his or her office; otherwise, the Vice President shall remain Acting President.

Related US Constitution Clause:
Whenever the Vice President and a majority of either the principal officers of the executive departments or of such other body as Congress may by law provide, transmit to the President pro tempore of the Senate and the Speaker of the House of Representatives their written declaration that the President is unable to discharge the powers and duties of his office, the Vice President shall immediately assume the powers and duties of the office as Acting President.

Thereafter, when the President transmits to the President pro tempore of the Senate and the Speaker of the House of Representatives his written declaration that no inability exists, he shall resume the powers and duties of his office unless the Vice President and a majority of either the principal officers of the executive department or of such other body as Congress may by law provide, transmit within four days to the President pro tempore of the Senate and the Speaker of the House of Representatives their written declaration that the President is unable to discharge the powers and duties of his office. Thereupon Congress shall decide the issue, assembling within forty-eight hours for that purpose if not in session. If the Congress, within twenty-one days after receipt of the latter written declaration, or, if Congress is not in session, within twenty-one days after Congress is required to assemble, determines by two-thirds vote of both Houses that the President is unable to discharge the powers and duties of his office, the Vice President shall continue to discharge the same as Acting President; otherwise, the President shall resume the powers and duties of his office.

Reason for Clause:
The original clause on Presidential succession in the US Constitution did not state who had the authority to declare a President unable to discharge his or her duties. While in office, President Wilson suffered a stroke that was concealed by his staff while he continued to serve as President, incapacitated. There was no way to force him to relinquish his authority. This unwieldy clause passed in a later amendment, resolves the problem.

Impact in the US:
The clause has never been used.

Impact on the European Union:
In the EU, there is no procedure to deal with the Commission President's inability to perform his or her duties.

Article 2 – Presidential Powers
Section 1

FEN Constitution Clause:
The President shall be Commander in Chief of the Armed Forces of the Federation and of any Armed Force of a Federation Nation when called into the actual service of the Federation. The President shall exercise executive authority over the executive departments and shall have power to grant reprieves and pardons for offences against the Federation, except for Impeachment.

Related US Constitution Clause:
The President shall be Commander in Chief of the Army and Navy of the United States, and of the Militia of the several States, when called into

the actual Service of the United States; he may require the Opinion, in writing, of the principal Officer in each of the executive Departments, upon any Subject relating to the Duties of their respective Offices, and he shall have Power to grant Reprieves and Pardons for Offences against the United States, except in Cases of Impeachment.

Reason for Clause:
This section delineates executive authority and command in wartime. The original thought was to have an Executive Council to direct the affairs of State. The eventual single executive was agreed to but some still wanted a council to advise the President consisting of the President of the Senate, the Chief Justice and the main Cabinet Ministers. Others claimed the Senate President and the Chief Justice had enough to do.

Impact in the US:
Although the powers granted to the Congress to declare war and the President to wage it have been blurred in recent years, the Founders believed that once the Congress declared war, the President had the ultimate and exclusive authority to wage it. Congress has issued no war declarations since World War II, but the US has still been involved in several conflicts, because Congress has passed specific resolutions authorizing war without a specific declaration.

The courts have given wide latitude to the President in dealing with threats to the nation, but have stated emphatically the he or she cannot act against the will of the Congress. Pardoning power was also assumed for the President since State governors already had the power. But argument centered on pardoning of treason, since a President who was treasonous could pardon his accomplices.

Impact on the European Union:
Since military operations in the European Union are under control of its member nations, the President of the EU Commission has no authority in military matters. The Commission President does, however, have authority over the Commission and the Executive organization of the EU but cannot pardon or reprieve offenses since criminal law is under control of member nations.

Section 2

FEN Constitution Clause:
The President shall have power to make treaties or executive agreements that shall have the force of law, provided two thirds of the Senators concur. With the concurrence of a majority of Senators, the President shall appoint Ambassadors, other public ministers and Consuls, Judges of the Supreme Court, and all other officers of the Federation whose appointments are not herein otherwise provided for, and are established by law. The Assembly, by law, may provide the power of appointment of subordinate officers to the President, his or her subordinates, or to the Judiciary without Senate approval.

Related US Constitution Clause:
He shall have Power, by and with the Advice and Consent of the Senate, to make Treaties, provided two thirds of the Senators present concur; and he shall nominate, and by and with the Advice and Consent of the Senate, shall appoint Ambassadors, other public Ministers and Consuls, Judges of the supreme Court, and all other Officers of the United States, whose Appointments are not herein otherwise provided for, and which shall be established by Law: but the Congress may by Law vest the Appointment of such inferior Officers, as they think proper, in the President alone, in the Courts of Law, or in the Heads of Departments.

Reason for Clause:
The Constitutional Convention had one group wanting a strong executive and another wanting a strong Congress. This clause was a compromise to maintain the balance of power between the President and the Congress. Early discussions gave the President authority to appoint the heads of Finance, War and Foreign Affairs unimpeded and the nomination of other officers with the approval of the Senate. After the delegates considered the Massachusetts State constitution, giving the Governor appointment authority and the State Senate approval authority, the entire discussion changed to adopt that procedure at the national level.

Appointment of Judges was considered differently. Early in the discussion, appointment of federal judges was to be left to the Congress but was whittled down to giving appointment authority only to the Senate as being the best judge of legal talent in their States. Then a proposal for the President to appoint justices to be approved by at least 1/3 of the Senate was brought up. Another proposal would allow appointment by the President unless 2/3 of the Senate disagreed. Finally, the above language was agreed upon.

Impact in the US:
Today, a congressional committee holds a hearing to question the Presidential appointee and recommends to the full Senate for confirmation on a majority vote. Treaties that have the force of law were originally to be approved by both houses of Congress. However, it was finally left to the Senate because treaties required a secrecy limiting the persons having access to them. The current language requires two thirds of the Senate to approve a treaty submitted by the President.

Impact on the European Union:
In the EU, The High Representative of the Union for Foreign Affairs and Security Policy is appointed by the European Council and approved by Parliament. The High Representative appoints EU ambassadors. Although foreign relations are handled by individual EU nations, the EU also has ambassadors in various countries.

As to the judiciary, each Member Nation appoints one judge, who must be approved by every other Member Nation, to the Court of Justice of the European Union.

Section 3

FEN Constitution Clause:
All Presidential appointments that, by law, must be approved by the Senate shall be voted on by the Senate within 90 days of submittal by the President or they shall be considered confirmed.

Related US Constitution Clause:
The President shall have Power to fill up all Vacancies that may happen during the Recess of the Senate, by granting Commissions which shall expire at the End of their next Session.

Reason for Clause:
From earlier clauses, we know that the Senate must approve certain Presidential appointments. During the early days of the US, the Congress was in recess for several months between sessions, and travel was measured in weeks rather than hours. Consequently, when senior officers resigned, calling the Senate into special session was not an option. The Constitutional Convention included this clause to allow the President to make appointments without Senate approval to keep the business of government moving.

Impact in the US:
These days, of course, Congress is in session year-round, making this clause unnecessary. The US Congress has frequently used its appointment approval authority as a political tool against the President, holding positions hostage by not bringing up their appointment for a vote, unless the President yielded to their wishes. This clause will eliminate that tool for the FEN Assembly.

Impact on the European Union:
In the EU, the President of the European Commission selects the 27 other members of the Commission based on suggestions of member states. The Commission must then be approved by Parliament. The Court of Justice of the European Union has one judge per Member State appointed by that member state for six years. A 7-person panel must approve each judge's appointment.

Article 3 – Presidential Responsibilities

FEN Constitution Clause:
The President, in the presence of the Assembly, shall annually address the People on the state of the Federation and recommend legislation to further Federation goals as expressed in the Preamble to this Constitution. The President shall have authority to call the Assembly into special session to address extraordinary problems. The President may adjourn the Assembly in case of disagreement between the two Houses on the time of adjournment. The President, as Head of State, shall receive Ambassadors and other public ministers, ensure that the

laws are executed in good faith, and shall commission all the officers of the Federation.

Related US Constitution Clause:
He shall from time to time give to the Congress Information of the State of the Union, and recommend to their Consideration such Measures as he shall judge necessary and expedient; he may, on extraordinary Occasions, convene both Houses, or either of them, and in Case of Disagreement between them, with Respect to the Time of Adjournment, he may adjourn them to such Time as he shall think proper; he shall receive Ambassadors and other public Ministers; he shall take Care that the Laws be faithfully executed, and shall Commission all the Officers of the United States.

Reason for Clause:
Delegates at the Constitutional Convention started out with a laundry list of duties the National Executive should have. This paragraph was a catchall for other things they wanted the Executive to do.
The idea behind the State of the Union address was to provide the Congress with the President's agenda for legislation at a time when most Congressmen needed a grasp of national issues facing the nation.

Impact in the US:
The first two Presidents delivered the State of the Union address in a speech to Congress. President Jefferson felt such a speech was too like the 'Speech from the Throne' British monarchs delivered to the House of Commons, discontinued it, and sent a written message instead. All Presidents followed the Jefferson procedure until Wilson revived the current speech to Congress, followed by all Presidents since.

In 1948, President Truman called Congress into special session to enact legislation they failed to enact during his term but promised to enact when a Republican President would be elected. That was the last time a special session was called, mainly because these days, Congress is in session all year long. The President's right to receive foreign dignitaries implies a broad power over foreign policy. 'Ensuring the laws are faithfully executed' prevents a President from stopping a member of the Executive Branch from executing a law, refusing to enforce a law or cancelling an appropriation.

Impact on the European Union:
The EU State of the Union speech is modeled after the US speech, is done annually, and is followed by a general debate on the political situation of the Union. The President of the EU Commission represents the EU to other nations and attends the meeting of the G8 along with EU members of the G8: France, Germany, Italy, and the United Kingdom. The EU has its own ambassadors to other nations along with the ambassadors of its member nations.

The President of the EU Commission oversees the Secretary General of the European Commission, who runs the operations of the EU.

Article 4 - Impeachment

FEN Constitution Clause:
The President, Vice President, Judges, and all civil officers of the Federation, as defined by law, shall be removed from office on Impeachment for, and conviction of, treason, bribery, perjury, abuse of authority, obstruction of justice, dereliction of duty, or other felonies.

Related US Constitution Clause:
The President, Vice President and all civil Officers of the United States, shall be removed from Office on Impeachment for, and Conviction of, Treason, Bribery, or other high Crimes and Misdemeanors.

Reason for Clause:
Any impeached and convicted official in the US is immediately removed from office and can be barred from holding any future federal office by the Senate, but no other punishment can be inflicted. However, the convicted official is still subject to trial in the courts on civil or criminal charges. An original proposal at the Constitutional Convention would have made the Chief Executive removable by the Legislature at the request of a majority of the State Legislatures. Others wanted the Legislature to have authority to remove the President at any time on a vote of no confidence.

After the impeachment process was decided, the Convention had to determine who would succeed an impeached and convicted President.

After considering the Chief Justice as a potential successor, the Convention developed the office of Vice President whose main function was to wait for the President to die, resign, become disabled or be removed.

Impact in the US: Nineteen federal officials have been impeached including three Presidents. Eight have been removed.

Impact on the European Union:
In the EU, the President of the European Commission can request the resignation of a Commissioner and the Parliament can dissolve the entire Commission including its President on a no-confidence vote.

Chapter III – The Judiciary
Article 1 – Federation Courts

FEN Constitution Clause:
The judicial power of the Federation shall be placed in one Supreme Court and in such subordinate courts as the Assembly may establish. The Judges, both of the Supreme and subordinate courts, shall hold their offices for life, unless removed by impeachment and conviction, or resignation, and shall receive for their services a compensation that shall not be diminished during their tenure even if the Assembly abolishes the court on which they serve.

Related US Constitution Clause:
The judicial Power of the United States, shall be vested in one supreme Court, and in such inferior Courts as the Congress may from time to time ordain and establish. The Judges, both of the supreme and inferior Courts, shall hold their Offices during good Behaviour, and shall, at stated Times, receive for their Services, a Compensation, which shall not be diminished during their Continuance in Office.

Reason for Clause:
During the Constitutional Convention, the delegates understood one of the weaknesses of the Articles of Confederation was the lack of a judiciary. Where no judiciary exists, there is no organization to interpret, pronounce and execute the law, decide controversies and

enforce rights. Some delegates did not want subordinate federal courts, claiming State courts would do just as well. Others responded that State courts could not be trusted to enforce national laws.

The agreement was to establish one mandated Supreme Court and authorize the legislature to create other subordinate courts as it saw fit.

Impact in the US:
The number of judges on the court is not addressed, but by law, the Supreme Court in the US has one Chief Justice and 8 Associate Justices. The US Congress has created district courts and appellate courts subordinate to the Supreme Court.

Since the Founding Fathers believed the Judiciary to be the weakest of the three branches, it needed protection from the encroachments of the other two. Lifetime appointments would allow the judges to decide without political pressure. The court could also check the power of the other two branches by ruling on the constitutionality of their actions. When two laws contradict each other, the courts' duty is to sort them out.

Impact on the European Union:
The European Court of Justice and the General Court are the judiciary of the European Union. Each member state appoints a judge to each court that is approved by all the member states. The 28 justices serve a renewable term of 6 years. The judges elect a President for a renewable term of three years.

Article 2 – Judicial Power, Jurisdiction and Trial by Jury
Section 1

FEN Constitution Clause:
The Judicial Power of the Federation of European Nations shall be over: all cases that arise under this Constitution, the laws of the Federation, and treaties and executive agreements made under its authority; all cases involving Ambassadors, Consuls and other ministers performing diplomatic functions; all cases of admiralty and maritime jurisdiction; controversies in which the Federation is a party; and controversies

between Federation Nations, between Citizens of different Federation Nations, and between Citizens of the same Federation Nation claiming property in a different Federation Nation.

Related US Constitution Clause:
The judicial Power shall extend to all Cases, in Law and Equity, arising under this Constitution, the Laws of the United States, and Treaties made, or which shall be made, under their Authority;—to all Cases affecting Ambassadors, other public Ministers and Consuls;—to all Cases of admiralty and maritime Jurisdiction;—to Controversies to which the United States shall be a Party;—to Controversies between two or more States;—between a State and Citizens of another State; —between Citizens of different States, —between Citizens of the same State claiming Lands under Grants of different States, and between a State, or the Citizens thereof, and foreign States, Citizens or Subjects.

The Judicial power of the United States shall not be construed to extend to any suit in law or equity, commenced or prosecuted against one of the United States by Citizens of another State, or by Citizens or Subjects of any Foreign State.

Reason for Clause:
Prior to deciding on a national judiciary, discussions at the Convention revolved around tortuous and convoluted systems involving the Senate, the State governments and State courts to resolve national issues. The first drafts limited the original judicial power of the federal courts to admiralty law, foreign law, national revenue, impeachments and national issues. Discussions expanded the jurisdiction to include laws passed by the National Legislature. The clause above finally settled the jurisdiction of the Judiciary Branch of the US government.

Impact in the US:
The 11th amendment was added later to remove the jurisdiction of the federal courts from cases between a State and a citizen of another State or by citizens of a foreign state. As a rule, a sovereign state must consent to its being sued, a concept known as sovereign immunity. The change maintained the sovereign immunity of the State to decide the applicability of its own laws against claims from citizens of another State or a foreign government.

And because of this change, the US Supreme Court has no authority to review decisions of State Supreme Courts on State Law. However, the Supreme Court does have jurisdiction over State courts on matters of federal law in their States. Any State law in contravention of a national law is void. The courts have also ruled that a State Legislature cannot annul a judiciary judgment of the US courts and cannot decide their jurisdiction.

To be considered a valid case for adjudication:
- the parties must have standing (a party has suffered harm from an action of another party),
- the case must not be moot (a judgment must have an effect),
- the case must be ripe (the action has caused actual not future harm), and,
- in civil actions, both parties must have something at stake.

Although the concept of judicial review of legislation to determine its constitutionality was not specifically given to the courts in the Constitution, the process of adjudication determines case law and precedent. No matter how well written a law, its effects remain obscure until its meaning is established in case law.

There have also been other limits placed on jurisdiction of the federal judiciary: For example,
- a foreign nation cannot be sued in federal court without its permission,
- A citizen of a US Territory cannot sue a citizen of another State in federal court, and
- the courts have no jurisdiction in criminal cases unless Congress has passed a law designating an act to be a federal crime.

Impact on the European Union:
In the EU, the European Court of Justice is the highest court. It interprets EU law and ensures its equal application across all EU member Nations.

Section 2

FEN Constitution Clause:
The Supreme Court shall have original jurisdiction in all cases affecting Ambassadors, Consuls, and other ministers performing diplomatic functions, and those in which a Federation Nation shall be a party. In all other cases under its authority, the Supreme Court shall have appellate jurisdiction, in law and fact, under such rules the Assembly shall make.

Related US Constitution Clause:
In all Cases affecting Ambassadors, other public Ministers and Consuls, and those in which a State shall be Party, the supreme Court shall have original Jurisdiction. In all the other Cases before mentioned, the supreme Court shall have appellate Jurisdiction, both as to Law and Fact, with such Exceptions, and under such Regulations as the Congress shall make.

Reason for Clause:
The Constitution sets the original jurisdiction (the court of first instance) for the Supreme Court. But it gives Congress the authority to define the Supreme Court's appellate jurisdiction. In effect, if Congress gives no appellate authority, the Court has none.

Impact in the US:
For example, the Supreme Court until 1889 could not receive appeals on federal criminal cases. Congress granted them that authority for capital cases in 1889 and for other federal crimes in 1891.

Impact on the European Union:
The European Court of Justice for the European Union has broad jurisdiction to interpret and apply provisions of the Treaties of the European Union. Under that authority, it can:
- determine whether a Member Nation has fulfilled its obligations under EU Law;
- rule on actions against the EU by a member Nation or individual;
- rule on the failure of an EU institution to act;

- decide on claims for compensation on non-contractual liability for damage to citizens caused by the EU; and,
- rule on points of law on judgments of the General Court (Court of first instance).

Section 3

FEN Constitution Clause:
The trial of all crimes, except in cases of impeachment, shall be by jury and be held in the Federation Nation where the alleged crime was committed. When the crime was not committed within any Federation Nation, the trial shall take place where the Assembly, by law, has directed.

Related US Constitution Clause:
The Trial of all Crimes, except in Cases of Impeachment, shall be by Jury; and such Trial shall be held in the State where the said Crimes shall have been committed; but when not committed within any State, the Trial shall be at such Place or Places as the Congress may by Law have directed.

Reason for Clause:
This right was in the English Magna Carta as a protection against oppression and tyranny by rulers. The jury requirement was to avoid a situation wherein those in power could use the courts as a political weapon. A trial is required to be held in the place where the alleged crime was committed to ensure the accused is not taken to a place where witnesses would not be available for his or her defense.

When debating this issue at the Constitutional Convention, the idea arose of a Bill of Rights to ensure special protection for personal liberties.

Impact in the US:
The Constitution was criticized after it was provided to the States for ratification because it did not provide the same protections for civil cases. Those were added in Amendment 7. The US Supreme Court has

decided this protection also applies to individuals on trial in State courts.

Impact on the European Union:
The treaties establishing the EU guarantee a defendant the right to a fair and public hearing but not a trial by jury. Moreover, each nation sets its own laws on criminal trials.

Article 3 - Treason
Section 1

FEN Constitution Clause:
Treason against the Federation of European Nations shall consist only in levying war against it or giving aid to its enemies. Conviction for treason requires the testimony of two witnesses to the same overt act or open confession in court.

Related US Constitution Clause:
Treason against the United States, shall consist only in levying War against them, or in adhering to their Enemies, giving them Aid and Comfort. No Person shall be convicted of Treason unless on the Testimony of two Witnesses to the same overt Act, or on Confession in open Court.

Reason for Clause:
In English law, there were five ways to be guilty of treason: levying war against the King, adhering to enemies of the King, imagining the Death of the King, counterfeiting, and fornicating with the Queen.
The Founding Fathers settled on only the first two.

Each phrase in the clause was debated, particularly 'aid and comfort' and 'same overt act' to ensure the charge of treason was not used to punish political opponents. Confession in open court was derived from the English Treason Act of 1695 and was included to prevent a forged or compelled written confession.

Treason against a State was also considered, but it was determined that Treason against a State would be treated as treason against the United States. In the end, the Convention defined the crime, fixed the proof for conviction and restrained Congress from extending its consequences beyond the traitor. The clause was placed under the Judiciary Section of the Constitution to ensure a military commission established by the President could not be used.

Impact in the US:
The Supreme Court has weighed in on this in three areas. First, to constitute a levying of war, there must be an assembly of men ready to conduct the treasonable purpose. Second, the two witnesses only must testify that an overt act occurred. Third, the witnesses do not have to prove intent or determine whether the act was treasonable.

Impact on the European Union:
The EU treaties do not mention treason. The crime only exists in the constitutions and laws of the member nations.

Section 2

FEN Constitution Clause:
The Assembly shall have power to prescribe the punishment for treason.

Related US Constitution Clause:
The Congress shall have Power to declare the Punishment of Treason, but no Attainder of Treason shall work Corruption of Blood, or Forfeiture except during the Life of the Person attainted.

Reason for Clause:
This clause gives Congress the sole right of determining the punishment for treason. At one time, in England, a traitor's descendants along with the traitor were punished because it was assumed the traitor had corrupted his lineage (blood), a concept not accepted these days. This clause removes the chances of that punishment in the US, and requires any property seized from the traitor returned to his or her heirs after the traitor's death.

Impact in the US: Very few treason trials have occurred in the US, most of them from World War II.

Impact on the European Union:
Although treason exists in the Constitutions of EU member nations, it is not mentioned in the EU treaties.

Chapter IV – Government Relationships
Article 1 – Full Faith and Credit

FEN Constitution Clause:
Each Nation shall recognize and enforce the public acts, records, and judicial proceedings of every other Nation. The Assembly, by law, may prescribe the manner in which such acts, records, and proceedings shall be proved, and their effect.

Related US Constitution Clause:
Full Faith and Credit shall be given in each State to the public Acts, Records, and judicial Proceedings of every other State. And the Congress may by general Laws prescribe the Manner in which such Acts, Records and Proceedings shall be proved, and the Effect thereof.

Reason for Clause:
This clause was expanded from a similar clause in the Articles of Confederation, giving Congress the authority to set the terms and manner of recognizing the public acts of the States.

Impact in the US:
The Supreme Court has ruled State courts may not reopen or reexamine a case decided by another State, but out of State judgments are still subject to the procedural laws of the State where they are to be enforced. On the other hand, foreign court judgments are examinable by US courts under laws of the US and States.

Impact on the European Union:
The EU's procedure on Recognition and Enforcement requires that a judgment in any EU country must be recognized in other EU countries without requiring any special procedure.

Article 2 – Obligations of Federation Nations
Section 1

FEN Constitution Clause:
A Federation Nation may not deprive the Citizens of another Federation Nation the privileges and immunities that its own Citizens enjoy, including but not limited to: protection by the government; the enjoyment of life and liberty; the right to travel through and reside in any other Federation Nation; the right to engage in commerce, agriculture, the professions or other occupation; the privilege of a writ requiring a Person under arrest to be brought before a judge; the right to institute action in any court; the right to obtain, hold and dispose of real and personal property; and, exemption from higher taxes than are paid by Citizens of the Federation Nation.

Related US Constitution Clause:
The Citizens of each State shall be entitled to all Privileges and Immunities of Citizens in the several States.

Reason for Clause:
Although appearing to be a clear statement, there were at least three interpretations of this clause. One group said the clause required Congress to treat all citizens equally, regardless of State of residence. Another group maintained that a person carried the rights and privileges from his home State when traveling to another State. Still another said the clause conferred citizens of each State United States citizenship.

Impact in the US:
The Supreme Court clarified it by saying the clause simply prohibits a State from discriminating against citizens of another State in favor of its own.

Impact on the European Union:
In the EU, 10 rights are granted to EU citizens:
- Voting and running for office in European and local elections;
- Making your voice heard;
- Free movement;

- Health;
- Consumer rights;
- Travel;
- Telecoms;
- Cross-border divorces and separations;
- Crime victims' rights and a fair trial; and,
- Information and guidance.

Section 2

FEN Constitution Clause:
A Person charged in any Nation with treason, felony, or other crime, who shall flee from justice and be found in another Nation, shall, on demand of the Head of Government from which he or she fled, be delivered up to the Nation having jurisdiction of the crime.

Related US Constitution Clause:
A Person charged in any State with Treason, Felony, or other Crime, who shall flee from Justice, and be found in another State, shall on Demand of the executive Authority of the State from which he fled, be delivered up, to be removed to the State having Jurisdiction of the Crime.

Reason for Clause:
'Other crime' includes all actions prohibited by State law, including misdemeanors. At the Constitutional Convention, southern State delegates wanted to add fugitive slaves as persons fleeing from criminal justice. A separate clause was added to mollify their concerns, since erased by the 13th Amendment.

Impact in the US:
The Supreme Court has ruled extradition can occur even if an indictment had not been issued, if the suspect fled the State to avoid prosecution. The fugitive can only defend himself against the crime in a court within the State that requested extradition. A fugitive may not challenge the authority of extradition, but can prevent it if clear evidence shows the fugitive was not in the State when the crime was committed. A State court cannot question the motives of the Governor

of the State requesting extradition. No extradition treaties are required between States.

Federal courts can also extradite fugitives.

Impact on the European Union:
The European Arrest Warrant simplified the extradition and judicial procedures for surrendering persons for criminal prosecution, custodial sentencing or spell in detention in the European Union. Because of it, EU countries can no longer refuse to surrender to another EU country their own citizens who are suspected of committing a serious crime in another EU country.

Section 3

FEN Constitution Clause:
Slavery or involuntary servitude, except as punishment for a crime for which the party has been duly convicted, shall not exist within the Federation or any place subject to its jurisdiction.

Related US Constitution Clause:
Neither slavery nor involuntary servitude, except as a punishment for crime whereof the party shall have been duly convicted, shall exist within the United States, or any place subject to their jurisdiction. Congress shall have power to enforce this article by appropriate legislation.

Reason for Clause:
This clause was not in the original Constitution since slavery was legal at the time and delegates from the southern States would have walked out of the Convention if their property were tampered with. In fact, the Fifth Amendment to the Constitution protected the slave owner, since it said that no person shall be deprived of life, liberty or property (i.e., slaves) without due process of law.

Impact in the US:
Several attempts by the non-slave holding States to ban slavery in the Congress were all ineffective. Subsequently, a series of rules were passed in Congress automatically tabling any petition to end slavery.

With the admission of Tennessee as the 16th State, the number of slave States and free States became equal. When new states were added after that time, a slave State and free State were added at the same time to maintain the power balance.

However, the Supreme Court's Dred Scott decision destroyed that balance by ruling a person could take their property (even slaves) into any US territory, thus making any future State a slave State. The election of Abraham Lincoln brought the nation to civil war as the slave States saw his election as a threat to their economy, culture and way of life.

After the war, the Congress passed the first of three Reconstruction Amendments that abolished slavery. Nevertheless, the southern States passed other laws, along with violence against blacks, enabling white Southerners to maintain freed slaves in a servile status.

Impact on the European Union:
In the European Union, the European Convention on Human Rights, Article 4, prohibits slavery or servitude or forced labor except for those in detention, military service, emergencies or normal civic obligations.

Section 4

FEN Constitution Clause:
A Person born in a Federation Nation and having one parent who was born in a Federation Nation, subject to its jurisdiction, or a Person naturalized within the Federation, is a Citizen of the Federation and the Nation wherein he or she resides. No Nation shall make or enforce any law that abridges the privileges or immunities of Citizens of the Federation, nor shall any Nation deprive any Person of life, liberty, or property, without due process of law, nor deny to any Person within its jurisdiction the equal protection of the laws.

Related US Constitution Clause:
All persons born or naturalized in the United States, and subject to the jurisdiction thereof, are citizens of the United States and of the State wherein they reside. No State shall make or enforce any law which shall abridge the privileges or immunities of citizens of the United States; nor

shall any State deprive any person of life, liberty, or property, without due process of law; nor deny to any person within its jurisdiction the equal protection of the laws.

Reason for Clause:
The clause above is not part of the original Constitution but the 14th Amendment to it. As part of Southern Reconstruction after the Civil War, it was intended to make former slaves, freed by the 13th Amendment, citizens of the US with the same rights as white citizens. It overturned the Supreme Court's Dred Scott decision stating blacks were property and had no rights that whites need respect. It specifically defines citizenship and prevents a State or local government from abridging those citizenship rights.

The phrase 'subject to its jurisdiction' excludes those persons born in the US whose parents are part of a nation's diplomatic community.

Impact in the US:
The clause has been used to affirm the citizenship of Native Americans and children of illegal immigrants, born on US soil. The issue has been revived over the term 'anchor babies', in which a pregnant foreign national comes to the US to purposely give birth to a child for automatic citizenship 'anchoring' the parent by providing him or her residency status.

Impact on the European Union:
The Treaty on the Functioning of the European Union declares every person who holds citizenship in a member nation to be a citizen of the EU.

Article 3 – Additions to the Federation and Control of Federation Property
Section 1

FEN Constitution Clause:
Foreign countries may be admitted by the Assembly into this Federation with the same status, rights, and obligations as existing Federation

Nations. However, no foreign country shall be admitted that is under the jurisdiction of any other Federation Nation or foreign country. Moreover, no Federation Nation shall be created by the merger of two or more Federation Nations, or parts of Federation Nations, without the consent of the Legislatures of the Nations concerned as well as of the Assembly.

Related US Constitution Clause:
New States may be admitted by the Congress into this Union; but no new State shall be formed or erected within the Jurisdiction of any other State; nor any State be formed by the Junction of two or more States, or Parts of States, without the Consent of the Legislatures of the States concerned as well as of the Congress.

Reason for Clause:
The Articles of Confederation allowed the admission of new States into the Confederation if agreed to by nine States. Upon its request, Canada could be admitted without approval of other States. The Treaty of Paris of 1783 ending the American Revolution, gave British lands west of the 13 State boundaries to the new American government. However, New York, Virginia and Maryland had claims over these lands. The Ordinance of 1787 set up a process for admitting these lands as States into the Union, becoming the inspiration for this clause in the Constitution.
The original language of this clause would have required 2/3 of each House to approve a new State's admission to the Union. There was also discussion whether a statement should be included that any new State should be equal to existing States in the Union. No statement was included, but all laws admitting new States had that statement included.

Discussions that centered on the authority of Congress to divide a State led to the final language.

Impact in the US:
Congress has placed restrictions on admission, which had to be accepted by the State prior to admission to the Union. However, the Supreme Court has voided any restriction on one State not applied to all States and any benefit a State enjoyed before joining the Union that was not enjoyed by all States. The only time a State was permitted to split itself from another State was during the Civil War, when counties in

western Virginia were accepted into the Union as the State of West Virginia after Virginia seceded from the Union.

Since that time, the Supreme Court has ruled no State could secede from the Union since the United States was a perpetual and indissoluble nation.

Impact on the European Union:
Any additions to the European Union must be approved by the European Parliament and all Member Nations.

Section 2

FEN Constitution Clause:
The Assembly shall have power to make all rules and regulations over the territory or other property belonging to the Federation; and nothing in this Constitution shall be so construed as to prejudice any claims of the Federation, or of any particular Federation Nation.

Related US Constitution Clause:
The Congress shall have Power to dispose of and make all needful Rules and Regulations respecting the Territory or other Property belonging to the United States; and nothing in this Constitution shall be so construed as to Prejudice any Claims of the United States, or of any particular State.

Reason for Clause:
During the Convention, one of the big issues to be decided was the ownership of western lands, those outside of traditional colonial boundaries that had been turned over to the new United States by Great Britain after the Revolution. Several colonies/States had claimed these lands as their own. The first attempt to resolve this issue was to provide the authority to determine ownership to the Supreme Court.

After discussion, the authority to determine claims was left to the Congress, stipulating the Constitution did not provide any rights to the State or the Federal Government as to ownership of these lands. This clause, known as the Property Clause, gives Congress the authority to dispose of and regulate the real and personal property of the US.

Impact in the US:
When the US acquired territory outside of its continental boundaries because of the Spanish American War, the Supreme Court had to decide on its management. It determined that federal property outside the States and the Federal District belonged to the US but was not part of the US. In effect, a territory cannot participate in the federal government until it becomes a State and is admitted into the union. On that basis, this clause gave Congress the authority to determine those parts of the Constitution applicable to them.

In a landmark case coming from this clause, the Supreme Court decided that private citizens could not purchase land from Native Americans, since they owned the land under aboriginal title and could only sell it to the federal government.

Impact on the European Union:
Under EU treaty, the property of the European Union is inviolable by member nations.

<u>Article 4 – Obligations of the Federation</u>

FEN Constitution Clause:
The Federation shall guarantee to every Federation Nation a Republican form of government, shall protect each of them against invasion, and upon request of its Legislature or of its Head of Government (when the Legislature cannot be convened), against domestic violence. The Assembly shall be the sole judge of whether a Nation has a republican form of government and shall confirm that judgment by acceptance or rejection of Delegates or Senators from that Nation by either House.

Related US Constitution Clause:
The United States shall guarantee to every State in this Union a Republican Form of Government, and shall protect each of them against Invasion; and on Application of the Legislature, or of the Executive (when the Legislature cannot be convened) against domestic Violence.

Reason for Clause:
The Founding Fathers believed in a Republic, where representatives, having a better understanding of the issues facing their constituents as well as national problems, could best develop solutions to those problems. At the time of the Convention, most delegates were concerned a monarchy would be set up in one of the States, that being the only alternative to a republic at the time. This clause, known as the Guarantee Clause, requires all States to be governed by the Republican principles of liberty, unalienable rights, sovereignty of the people, minority rights under majority rule and consent of the governed.

However, none of these principles appears in or is explained in the Constitution. However, in parts of the Constitution, the principles are implied. For example, Article 7 required the ratification of the Constitution by a vote of the people illustrating their sovereignty and the principle of 'consent of the governed'. And since only 9 of 13 States were required to adopt the new Constitution, it showed that a minority could not frustrate the will of the majority.

Impact in the US:
Whether a State had a Republican government was a question clarified by the Supreme Court in 1849 when it stated that the issue was political and not judicial and therefore must be resolved by Congress and not the courts. This decision led to the Congressional actions after the Civil War when Congress set standards for the seceded States to reenter the Union.

While all agreed with the duty of the national government to protect the States from invasion, an insurrection or rebellion was a different matter. Some delegates feared the power of Congress to insert itself into the affairs of States. That is why a State must ask the federal government for assistance in cases of insurrection or rebellion.

The Insurrection Act of 1807, known as the Posse Comitatus Act, prevented the President from unilaterally using the military to put down lawlessness, insurrection and rebellion and required the State to request federal action of the President. Normally, a State should be able to handle its own internal violence with the resources of the Police and

National Guard. The Insurrection Act was almost used in the Detroit riots of 1967, but the Governor of Michigan did not declare a state of Insurrection, and therefore the President could not act.

Impact on the European Union:
Every nation in the EU has signed the European Convention for the Protection of Human Rights and Fundamental Freedoms of 1950, which means only democratic states, respecting human rights, can apply for membership.

Chapter V – Amendments to this Constitution

FEN Constitution Clause:
This Constitution can be amended in two ways. First, whenever two thirds of both Houses shall deem it necessary, the Assembly shall propose Amendments to this Constitution; or, secondly, when the Legislatures of two thirds of Federation Nations shall call for a Convention to propose Amendments. In either case, the Amendments shall be valid to all intents and purposes, as part of this Constitution, when ratified by either the Legislatures of three fourths of Federation Nations, or by Conventions in three fourths thereof, as determined by the Assembly. However, no Federation Nation, without its consent, shall be deprived of its equal representation in the Senate. Once a Federation Nation ratifies or rejects an Amendment, the action is final. Any Amendment not ratified within ten years after its submittal to Federation Nations by the Assembly for approval shall be considered rejected.

Related US Constitution Clause:
The Congress, whenever two thirds of both Houses shall deem it necessary, shall propose Amendments to this Constitution, or, on the Application of the Legislatures of two thirds of the several States, shall call a Convention for proposing Amendments, which, in either Case, shall be valid to all Intents and Purposes, as Part of this Constitution, when ratified by the Legislatures of three fourths of the several States, or by Conventions in three fourths thereof, as the one or the other Mode of Ratification may be proposed by the Congress; Provided that no Amendment which may be made prior to the Year One thousand eight

hundred and eight shall in any Manner affect the first and fourth Clauses in the Ninth Section of the first Article; and that no State, without its Consent, shall be deprived of its equal Suffrage in the Senate.

Reason for Clause:
The first idea of amending the Constitution at the Constitutional Convention did not give a role to Congress. In fact, some did not see a need to amend the Constitution at all. Others argued that some defects would be quickly evident and a process to correct them would be necessary. The first suggestion was to allow two-thirds of the States to petition Congress to call a Convention. Then they added a provision for Congress to propose Amendments with State approval.

The small States were concerned an Amendment would be proposed to take away their equal representation in the Senate and a provision was added to allay their fears (but that provision can also be amended).

Impact in the US:
Since ratification of the Constitution, over 11,000 Amendments have been proposed in Congress. Only thirty-three have been approved by Congress and sent to the States for ratification, of which 27 were ratified. The first 10 Amendments, called the Bill of Rights, were adopted at one time soon after the Constitution itself was ratified. Normally, Amendments are passed as Joint Resolutions of both the House and Senate. Unlike other Congressional actions, however, the Supreme Court has ruled the President has no role in this process and cannot veto or approve an Amendment passed by Congress.

The other method of Amendment described, the States' initiative, happens when two-thirds of State legislatures request a convention that Congress must convene for the States to propose Amendments.
In effect, this method would convene another Constitutional Convention. The idea strikes fear into the hearts of some political leaders, thinking any convention could stray from the original issues involved and end up with a wholesale revision of the Constitution. Because of this fear, no convention has ever been called since any resolutions from the States to amend the Constitution are usually considered by Congress if enough States show an interest in a subject.

The Constitution also provides two methods for State ratification of Amendments: Legislature approval or State Conventions. All the Amendments to date have been passed by State Legislatures save one: the Repeal of Prohibition Amendment that specifically required State Conventions to ratify or disapprove it.

Recent Amendments have time stipulations in the Congressional Resolutions but that has not always been the case. Early Amendments are still awaiting ratification and have no time limit for that purpose. In fact, the 27th Amendment was proposed in 1789 and was not ratified by the required number of States until 1992.

Impact on the European Union:
In the EU, there is an ordinary and simplified procedure to amend the Treaties establishing and governing the EU. However, all Member Nations must approve any change to the treaties.

Chapter VI – Supremacy, Establishment, Allegiance and Definition of Person
Article 1 - Debts

FEN Constitution Clause:
All debts contracted before the adoption of this Constitution shall be as valid within the Federation under this Constitution as under the European Union.

Related US Constitution Clause:
All Debts contracted and Engagements entered into, before the Adoption of this Constitution, shall be as valid against the United States under this Constitution, as under the Confederation.

Reason for Clause:
This clause was meant to ensure no debts incurred by States under the Articles of Confederation would be abrogated. Those delegates who were financially responsible ensured this clause was in the Constitution to reassure European creditors that the new government stood upon a sound financial base.

Impact in the US: The issue of debt centered on the money borrowed by each State to fund its military activities during the Revolution. Some States (mostly northern) wanted the new federal government to assume those state debts. But other States (mostly southern) who had paid back part of their debts objected to bailing out other States who had not.

The first great compromise under the new Constitution was the passage of a law allowing the federal government to assume the debts of all the States, satisfying Northern needs. In return, the capital of the United States was to be established between Maryland and Virginia, satisfying Southern needs.

Article 2 - Supremacy

FEN Constitution Clause:
This Constitution and the laws of the Federation and all treaties and executive agreements which shall be enacted under it, shall be the supreme law of the Federation and the Judges in every Nation shall be bound thereby, anything in a Nation's Constitution or laws to the contrary notwithstanding.

Related US Constitution Clause:
This Constitution, and the Laws of the United States which shall be made in Pursuance thereof; and all Treaties made, or which shall be made, under the Authority of the United States, shall be the supreme Law of the Land; and the Judges in every State shall be bound thereby, any Thing in the Constitution or Laws of any State to the Contrary notwithstanding.

Reason for Clause:
This clause is known as the Supremacy Clause because it makes the Constitution and all laws and treaties made under it the supreme law of the land governing the decisions of all courts including State and local courts. Under the Articles of Confederation, States routinely ignored laws passed by the Confederation Congress. Although delegates wanted to strengthen the national government, some feared the federal government would make slaves of the States if a supremacy clause were included.

After an attempt to develop a list of areas where federal power would be limited, delegates gave up and agreed on the above clause.

Impact in the US:
In its effect, the clause states that any State law conflicting with federal law is void and all State Constitutions are subordinate to federal law. The States also have no authority to control the actions of federal institutions within their States nor can they tax them or their property. The Supreme Court has since decided that a State court has no jurisdiction to prohibit a judgment of a US court and the Congress has specific authorities that the State cannot interfere with.

Impact on the European Union:
In the EU, the Court of Justice has determined EU law is supreme over national Constitutions and laws.

Article 3 - Allegiance

FEN Constitution Clause:
The Senators and Delegates of the Federation, National Legislatures of its Member Nations and all executive and judicial officers both of the Federation and of its Member Nations shall be bound by oath or affirmation to support this Constitution, but no religious test shall ever be required as a qualification to any office under the Federation. The Assembly shall determine the wording of the oath but no religious book or symbol shall be required to administer the oath.

Related US Constitution Clause:
The Senators and Representatives before mentioned, and the Members of the several State Legislatures, and all executive and judicial Officers, both of the United States and of the several States, shall be bound by Oath or Affirmation, to support this Constitution; but no religious Test shall ever be required as a Qualification to any Office or public Trust under the United States.

Reason for Clause:
The purpose of the clause was to ensure governmental officials at all levels bought into the new Constitution. Some objected saying it

intruded on State sovereignty and requested that federal officers should swear to preserve State Constitutions also. Others contended federal officials would never have a role in enforcing State law but that State governments would have an essential role in enforcing federal laws. They also stated without the oath, State judges might favor their own State laws if they conflicted with national law.

Impact in the US:
Consequently, all elected officials, and military and civilian officers and judges at all governmental levels in the US are required to take the following oath, passed by the First Congress:

I, [name], do solemnly swear (or affirm) that I will support and defend the Constitution of the United States against all enemies, foreign and domestic; that I will bear true faith and allegiance to the same; that I take this obligation freely, without any mental reservation or purpose of evasion; and that I will well and faithfully discharge the duties of the office on which I am about to enter. [So, help me God.]

Note the last four words. Since no religious test can be used to exclude or include a person from office, those last words are not required to be said, but most office holders say them.

Impact on the European Union:
Officers of the EU take an oath to respect the EU treaties but no comparative oath is required of Member Nation officers to respect the EU treaties.

Article 4 – Definition of Natural Person

FEN Constitution Clause:
The rights protected by this Constitution are intended to be the rights of natural Persons. Consequently, the words People, Person, or Citizen as used in this Constitution do not include corporations, limited liability companies, or other corporate entities established by the laws of any Nation, the Federation, or any foreign country. Such corporate entities are subject to such regulation as the People, through their elected National and Federation representatives, deem reasonable and

otherwise consistent with the powers of the Assembly and the Nations under this Constitution.

Related US Constitution Clause:
No reference

Impact in the US:
The 14th Amendment has been interpreted by the courts to provide constitutional protections to corporations as persons. Because of this, a corporation can own property, enter into contracts, can sue in court and be sued and prosecuted under civil and criminal law. In effect, a corporation cannot be deprived of its constitutional rights just as a human being cannot. Current US law maintains that in any Act of Congress, unless indicating otherwise, the word person includes corporations, companies, associations, firms, partnerships, societies and joint stock companies as well as individuals.

Many in the US have objected to this interpretation as providing a huge amount of power to corporate entities over and above an ordinary individual. The FEN language above provides a statement limiting that power to laws passed by the Assembly and is not a strict constitutional protection.

Impact on the European Union:
Current European law, like US law, considers corporations to also have legal personhood.

Chapter VII – Ratification and the European Union

FEN Constitution Clause:
The ratification by the People of eighteen Nations of the European Union in separate referendums shall be sufficient for the establishment of this Constitution among the Nations ratifying it. Any Nation that has not ratified this Constitution by the date it is established may only be admitted to the Federation under the provisions of Chapter IV, Article 3 of this Constitution.

Related US Constitution Clause:
The Ratification of the Conventions of nine States, shall be sufficient for the Establishment of this Constitution between the States so ratifying the Same.

Reason for Clause:
Although some delegates thought a popular ratification of the new Constitution unnecessary, the majority said a popular vote would provide the best authority. Although a majority of seven States was thought to be the number needed for ratification, others thought more should be required to ensure legitimacy. Ratification by nine states was eventually agreed upon, although some wanted a unanimous approval since the Articles of Confederation had been unanimous.

Impact in the US:
Three days after the delegates to the Constitutional Convention approved the document, it was provided to the Congress under the Articles of Confederation. After much debate, the Congress voted to provide the Constitution to the States for their review without either endorsing or opposing the document. Over the next nine months, the Constitution was debated in newspapers and speeches all throughout the States.

Conventions were held in each State to decide the document's fate. By the end of 1787, Delaware, Pennsylvania and New Jersey had all ratified it but the required ninth State, New Hampshire, did not ratify it until June 1788. The Congress chose March 4, 1789 as the day for beginning proceedings under the new Constitution. Virginia and New York ratified it before that date and North Carolina and Rhode Island after.

After the date was selected, the State legislatures were asked to elect their Senate members and set up the election of representatives. The election of the President would then take place and the Constitution executed.

Impact on the European Union:
In contrast, the EU treaties had to be signed by all EU member nations.

Road to the Decision

The Convention in Philadelphia

T he Constitutional Convention delegates in Philadelphia agreed to provide the finished document to the Congress of the Confederation for submittal to the States for ratification, specifically by a convention of delegates in each State. When 9 States had ratified it, the Congress of the Confederation would set a day when electors would be appointed by the ratifying States, a day when the electors would assemble to vote for President and a time and place for beginning the new government. After that, the Senators and Representatives would be elected and convene in the time and place determined and begin the new government by counting the votes for President, who would begin to execute the Constitution.

George Washington as President of the Convention, transmitted the document to the Congress stating:

> "The friends of our country have long seen and desired that the power of making war, peace, and treaties, that of levying money, and regulating commerce, and the correspondent executive and judicial authorities, should be fully and effectually vested in the General Government of the Union; but the impropriety of delegating such extensive trust to one body of men is evident: hence results the necessity of a different organization.
>
> It is obviously impracticable in the Federal Government of these States to secure all rights of independent sovereignty to each, and yet provide for the interest and safety of all.
>
> Individuals entering into society must give up a share of liberty to preserve the rest.
>
> The magnitude of the sacrifice must depend as well on situation and circumstance, as on the object to be obtained.

It is at all times difficult to draw with precision the line between those rights which must be surrendered, and those which may be preserved; and, on the present occasion, this difficulty was increased by a difference among the several States as to their situation, extent, habits, and particular interests.

In all our deliberations on this subject, we kept steadily in our view that which appears to us the greatest interest of every true American, the consolidation of our Union, in which is involved our prosperity, felicity, safety—perhaps our national existence.

This important consideration, seriously and deeply impressed on our minds, led each State in the Convention to be less rigid on points of inferior magnitude than might have been otherwise expected; and thus, the Constitution which we now present is the result of a spirit of amity, and of that mutual deference and concession, which the peculiarity of our political situation rendered indispensable.

That it will meet the full and entire approbation of every State is not, perhaps, to be expected; but each will, doubtless, consider, that had her interest alone been consulted, the consequences might have been particularly disagreeable or injurious to others; that it is liable to as few exceptions as could reasonably have been expected, we hope and believe; that it may promote the lasting welfare of that Country so dear to us all, and secure her freedom and happiness, is our most ardent wish."

The same letter could apply to the European Union. But the first question of the first part of this roadmap is: How did the United States of America get to this position?

On March 25, 1785, delegates from Maryland and Virginia met at George Washington's home to deal with navigational rights on waterways between the two States, the Congress of the Confederation being unable or unwilling to do so. Three days later, the conference adjourned with a report, later approved by the Virginia and Maryland legislatures, regulating commerce, fishing and navigation on the Potomac and Pocomoke Rivers and the Chesapeake Bay.

The Virginia Legislature, on January 21, 1786, called for an inter-State convention to address trade barriers.   On September 11, 5 State delegates met at Annapolis to discuss a method to establish rules for commerce between the States. Delegates appointed by 4 other States either arrived too late or did not attend at all, while 4 States did not appoint delegates. Three days later, the convention adjourned with a call to all States to send delegates to a convention the following May to amend the Articles of Confederation.

On February 21, 1787, the Congress of the Confederation formally called a constitutional convention to revise the Articles of Confederation.

After a quorum was reached on May 25, the Convention came to order and Washington was elected Presiding Officer. Over the next days, plans for structuring the federal government were submitted.

- The Virginia Plan submitted by Edmund Randolph set up a bicameral legislature. The lower house would be elected by population. The upper House would be elected by the lower House. The Legislature would elect the President. Larger States like Virginia would have more influence.
- That same day, Charles C. Pinckney set forth his own plan for a bicameral legislature like the Virginia Plan but it was not debated.
- On June 15, William Paterson submitted the New Jersey Plan (the Small State Plan) giving each State only 1 vote like the Congress of the Confederation.
- Three days later, Alexander Hamilton submitted his plan, the British Plan, which established a bicameral legislature consisting of one house elected by the people for a three-year term and the other house having life terms selected by electors elected by the people. The legislature would elect a Governor who would also serve for life.

Washington appointed a Committee of eleven on July 2 to work out a compromise on the legislative plans. The committee reported on July 16 a compromise plan giving proportional representation by population in the House of Representatives and equal representation in the Senate for each State. On July 24, the Committee of Detail was appointed to draft a Constitution to reflect the decisions agreed to at that point.

Come August 6, the Committee of Detail proposed a 23-article constitution. Separate Committees of Eleven were established over the next weeks to deal with the issue of federal assumption of State debt, the role of State militia, federal tax authority, regulation of slavery importation and trade and navigation.

A Committee on Leftover Business was tasked on August 31 to settle parts of the Constitution postponed or not acted on. This Committee met from September 1-8 to develop the method of choosing the executive, his term of office, duties and removal. On September 8, a Committee of Style and Arrangement was selected to prepare the final draft, submitted on September 12, composed of seven articles, a preamble, closing endorsement and proposed transmittal letter to Congress. Three days later, the Constitution was unanimously approved, each State having one vote.

However, before the Constitution was accepted as the basis for the federal government, public debate and voting would have to approve its adoption. The Congress accepted the document on September 20 and for two days argued whether the Convention had exceeded its authority, since it had been directed to amend the Articles of Confederation not create a new document. After deciding to drop the argument, the Congress, on September 28, directed the State legislatures to call conventions in each State.

Nine States had to approve the document for it to be active. Since the Convention had conducted its business in secrecy, no minutes officially kept, the conventions were the place where the new government was debated, State by State. The conventions insured that the authority for the Constitution came from the will of the electorate. If conducted in State legislatures, amendments would have been attached which would have made it difficult to reach a final agreement.

Those who approved the new Constitution (Federalists) debated with those opposed (Anti-Federalists) in newspapers, pamphlets and meetings. The Antifederalists claimed the delegates had exceeded their authority, they represented only the wealthy and gave too much power to the central government. In a series of published essays, Alexander Hamilton, James Madison and John Jay responded to the Anti-Federalists point by point. These essays were published in two volumes, known today as the Federalist Papers, analyzing each part of the Constitution.

But the most serious problem brought up by the Anti group was the lack of a Bill of Rights. After the Federalists agreed that the first task of the new government would be to amend the Constitution to provide a Bill of Rights, any significant opposition dwindled. Ratification took 10 months, with the first State, Delaware, approving in a unanimous 30-0 vote on December 7, 1787. Massachusetts wavered until the promise of a Bill of Rights broke the deadlock.

New Hampshire was the 9th State to ratify on June 21st 1788 to put the new government in motion. The remaining States less Rhode Island followed. Faced with treatment as a foreign nation, Rhode Island finally ratified the document by two votes. Congress, on September 13, set the date and place for the first meeting of the new government and the Presidential election.

On February 4, under the rules of the Constitution, the Electoral College met in each State to cast its votes for President and Vice President. Only 10 States cast votes because New York had not appointed its electors and North Carolina and Rhode Island had not ratified the Constitution.

The first Congress under the Constitution met in New York City on March 4, 1789 with 22 Senators and 50 Representatives elected, but without a valid quorum. On April 1, the House convened with a quorum and elected a Speaker, followed by the Senate on April 6. That day, the House and Senate met in joint session, opened the electoral ballots and certified that Washington had been elected President and John Adams, Vice President. Washington was inaugurated on April 30, 1789.

The Congress adopted 12 Amendments to the Constitution on September 25 and sent them to the States for ratification. Ten of this 12 are known as the Bill of Rights. John Jay as Chief Justice convened the first session of the Supreme Court on February 2, 1790. And the rest, as they say...is history.

Reforming the European Union

The Constitution for the Federation of European Nations requires each nation ratifying it to leave the European Union. Because the Federation is a political and not just a commercial union of sovereign states, it is impossible for a nation to be part of both simultaneously. Consequently, Article 50 of the Lisbon Treaty must be invoked by those ratifying the Constitution when the FEN is declared in operation. How does this work?

New ground must be plowed since no nation has left the EU once joining. Great Britain is in the process of leaving but it has yet to invoke this article. The text of Article 50 follows:

"1. Any Member State may decide to withdraw from the Union in accordance with its own constitutional requirements.

2. A Member State which decides to withdraw shall notify the European Council of its intention. In the light of the guidelines provided by the European Council, the Union shall negotiate and conclude an agreement with that State, setting out the arrangements for its withdrawal, taking account of the framework for its future relationship with the Union. That agreement shall be negotiated in accordance with Article 218(3) of the Treaty on the Functioning of the European Union. It shall be concluded on behalf of the Union by the Council, acting by a qualified majority, after obtaining the consent of the European Parliament.

3. The Treaties shall cease to apply to the State in question from the date of entry into force of the withdrawal agreement or, failing that, two years after the notification referred to in paragraph 2, unless the European Council, in agreement with the Member State concerned, unanimously decides to extend this period.

4. For the purposes of paragraphs 2 and 3, the member of the European Council or of the Council representing the withdrawing Member State shall not participate in the discussions of the European Council or Council or in decisions concerning it. A qualified majority shall be defined in accordance with Article 238(3)(b) of the Treaty on the Functioning of the European Union.

5. If a State which has withdrawn from the Union asks to rejoin, its request shall be subject to the procedure referred to in Article 49."
One of the main parts of the Treaty of Lisbon that governs the EU hopes for "an ever closer union among the peoples of Europe." This phrase first occurs in the Preamble to the 1957 Treaty that established the EU. Since the Federation of European Nations certainly meets the desires of that phrase, there should be no objection to nations leaving the EU to more fully merge. In fact, in June 2014, the EU stated that "the concept of ever closer union allows for different paths of integration for different countries, allowing those that want to deepen integration to move ahead, while respecting the wish of those who do not want to deepen any further". A Europe that would embrace the FEN and leave the EU with no overlap among countries would certainly meet this goal.

What would happen and which countries would like to join the FEN? Since it appears the EU proponents overreached in making an economic union a political one, joining the FEN would require the joiner to give up more sovereignty than the EU requires. So...is there even a possibility of any country wanting to join the FEN if they object to being a part of the EU? For example, Marine Le Pen had pledged to hold a Frexit referendum if she is elected President of France next year. Since the main supporters and founders of the EU were France and Germany, a Frexit would certainly end the EU. And after the Netherlands rejected a Ukraine-EU treaty, it could also be eager to leave the EU.

Additional countries pondering referendums are Italy, Austria, Finland and Hungary. Although Germany is encouraging the stand that Britain could retain an associated relationship with the EU, other EU nations are against giving EU privileges to the Brits after withdrawal. Italy lately warned the EU to change its course to avoid a total collapse while Poland's foreign minister said Brexit shows the need to reform the EU.

The current concept is not popular. Even Turkey, once desirous of joining the EU proclaimed that the 'Crusader Union Falls Apart." A March April 2016 poll indicated the majority of those polled in Italy and France wanted a referendum on the EU but oddly even those wanting a referendum would not vote to leave the EU. In any case, anti-EU parties are calling for referendums next year.

The main reasons stem from discontent over austerity programs and nationalism spurred by Islamophobia and anti-immigration.
Here is the status, country by country:

Netherlands. Violent protests have been generated by the far right Dutch Party for Freedom against asylum seekers and rising racism. This despite the Netherlands being a founding EU member holding the EU Presidency at present. A poll in June indicated 54 percent wanted a referendum on leaving the EU. Although a referendum requires a constitutional amendment needing 2/3 of Parliament to be ratified, a recent law requires only 300,000 signatures on a petition to trigger a non-binding referendum.

France. Euroscepticism is greater in France than in Britain, A struggling economy and anti-immigration feelings have turned public opinion against the EU. Prior to the Brexit vote, a survey found that 61 percent of French voters have an unfavorable view of the EU, and a clear majority is opposed to an 'ever closer union'. Some French believe the EU has been taken over by faceless technocrats. The Republican party in France has called for eliminating the European Commission and launching a confederation of nation states. In effect, Europe needs to change to reform or end the EU.

Italy. A referendum was called for by the Northern League, but the government said there is no prospect of an exit. On another tack, the Five Star Movement has called for a return to the lire.

Austria. The Far Right Freedom Party want to make the EU strictly an economic free trade union. Any further move toward centralization is anathema to them. They have called for the resignations of the European Commission President, and President of Parliament along with a return of power to national parliaments, the end of border free travel, and the right of each nation to control its immigration.

Germany. The EU remains popular in one of the major founders of the Union. But the open border policy of the German Chancellor has caused concern in other nations.

Poland. Hundreds of thousands of Poles working in Britain are worried about their status after Brexit. The government has relied on Britain to serve as a check on the centralizing aspirations of Germany and France within the EU. It blames the EU leadership for failing to keep one of its most critical members, does not want closer integration and promotes a new EU treaty to end the dream of a Federation and loosen ties. However, there is no sentiment of leaving since Poland has only benefitted from its membership including a modern road network, fast trains and farm subsidies.

Denmark. The populist Danish People's Party stressed that a leave referendum should be postponed until Britain has agreed to a settlement with the EU, hoping to receive the same deal Britain gets. That could entice the EU to deal strongly with Britain. Negative Danish votes against the Maastricht treaty, joining the Euro and its opt-out from certain EU rules foretell a vote to leave the EU if called.

Finland. The Populist Finns party had called for an EU referendum. What is needed is either deeper integration or leaving the EU. But the Prime Minister indicated the Brexit was a disappointment.

Sweden. The Anti-immigrant Sweden Democrats called for a referendum, but the mainstream parties still favor EU membership. A poll after Brexit showed a majority of Swedes favored EU membership. Opposition parties maintain that the EU handling of immigration, finance and trade has been below par.

Hungary. Despite being a critic of the EU, Hungary has no immediate intention to leave. The Prime Minister stated Hungary would have difficulty thriving outside the EU. However, he did not believe closer integration was possible. It will however proceed with a referendum on the migrant quota assigned by the EU.

Is a FEN possible?

Perhaps in one of three ways.

One, a single country would take the lead in calling for a FEN. Which one would it be? It would have to be a founder of the EU, that used the Euro, and was large enough to be confident in its role in the FEN and willing to give up its sovereignty. My guess: Germany, even though most other European nations would find it difficult to form a political union with a nation two times before has tried to unify Europe by force. But the same could be said for France.

Second is that several small countries could start the FEN to counter the power of the larger countries. They would most likely be contiguous. The Nordic countries of Denmark, Norway, Sweden plus Finland could unite. Add to them the Baltic countries and you would have a FEN of 26 Million people with 1.4 Trillion GDP. Russia's aggressive actions might also encourage the former Soviet bloc of Poland, the Czech Republic, Slovakia, Hungary, Romania and Bulgaria to merge, creating a 91-million-person state, greater than the population of Germany or France.

The third way would be like the American model. One country would submit a FEN constitution in whatever form to the EU Parliament and recommend it be sent to all the EU nations. Obviously, there would need to be strong political backing for such a move from major countries.

Of course, all of this is supposition. It may never come to pass and the EU may weather this storm of economic and immigration chaos. But to really become a player in the world, Europe at some time will need to be more than just a trade union.